Unable
to
Resist

Unable to

to

Resist

WHEN YOU'RE SUDDENLY A CAREGIVER
and It's Really Not Your Gift

Kay Nell Miller

You feel overwhelmed. You feel anxiety. You feel isolated. But you are not alone.

A phone call changed Kay Nell Miller's life forever. One minute she was a confident, bold entrepreneur, the next minute she became a caregiver for her mom for the next thirteen years. She wanted to care for her mom after a stroke—but she didn't know how, but God saw her through it all.

Have *you* suddenly been called to be a caregiver?
You can be confident, free from stress and anxiety, and fearless.

Kay Nell Miller is a Podcaster, Author, Pianist, Bible Teacher, and Creator of Waves of Mercy non-denominational Christian women's retreats. She encourages women from all walks of life in their relationship with God and each other. She also a one-on-one Coach for Christ-centered caregivers.

Kay Nell Miller married the love of her life, Phil, in 1974. She loves swimming, laughing, and living near the Oregon coast range with wildlife abounding. They are unable to resist connecting with their son, Jordan, daughter-in-love, Nicole, and granddaughter, Laurel Elizabeth. The beach Kay Nell's favorite place to relax, unwind, and experience God.

Get in touch

Facebook Private Group: Authentic Caregiving

Facebook Page: Kay Nell Miller Authentic Caregiving –
schedule a free 15-minute caregiver consult

Instagram: Authentic_Caregiving

YouTube: Authentic Caregiving with Kay Nell Miller

UNABLE TO RESIST:
WHEN YOU'RE SUDDENLY A CAREGIVER
AND IT'S REALLY NOT YOUR GIFT

Copyright © 2021 Kay Nell Miller

Published by Bosque Publishing, LLC
PO Box 728, Banks, OR 97106

Cover and interior page layout: theBookDesigners,
Alan Hebel and Ian Koviak

Developmental Editor: James N. Watkins,
author, speaker, beloved child of God

Copy Editor: Kali Connelly

Paperback ISBN: 978-1-736-3296-0-3
Ebook ISBN: 978-1-7363296-1-0

First Edition: October 2021

Dedication

This book is dedicated to my son, Jordan:

You are always fresh from the hand of God. You listen to me, encourage me, challenge me, inspire me, and make me laugh out loud. You told me I could write and passed on tools to help me start. You watched me as a caregiver for your grandma, loved her, and never complained.

You are more than I ever dreamed. May your faith continue growing, asking God the hard questions and helping others find their way, too. May you never quit. You are my greatest joy and every day I'm cheering you onward. I'll be waiting for you on the other side one day, and we'll both laugh out loud together, and kiss the top of your head.

Contents

Few Travelers

Walking Home

I want to walk into your home again and
Inhale the familiar
I want to open your refrigerator door,
gazing at what's inside
Then close it again
I want to see Spuddy, tearing
Down the sidewalk, leash-free
I want to see you walking an easy
Gait behind the lawn mower, magically
Creating free, fresh, soothing aromas
I want to saunter in Christmas Eve, my
Arms full of you, the big gray kettle simmering with
Hot, comforting soup, a platter of fresh bread and over
One hundred colorful popcorn balls
I want things to be as they were: full of hope, drunk
With passion and possibilities
I want to cuddle on your lap
in the old rocking chair and
Hear you singing and speaking
comforting words into my ear
I want to be standing in the shade of
You and your love again.

by *Kay Nell Miller*

xiii

Introduction

Courage is when you are so afraid, yet you move forward anyway. There is emotional courage, spiritual courage, moral courage, intellectual courage, and social courage. All of these are covered in these pages, and vulnerable stories highlighting them all.

... *"lion, king of animals, who won't turn aside for anything"*...
PROVERBS 30:30 (NLT)

This book has been burning in my soul for ten years. Although I began intense caregiving on the eighth day of early retirement, I entered it silently kicking and screaming, "Nooooo!.." Even still, I was unable to resist becoming a caregiver for my mom, Kathryn, for thirteen years--through two strokes and nine transient ischemic attacks (TIAs). It took awkward vulnerability, crying, fearless courage, emotional outbursts, consistent endurance, lack of sleep, and an intimate walking with God. I trampled down brush and stumbled over logs for answers during this time. The result is a step-by-step path that will equip you in every aspect of caregiving.

Hundreds of caregivers struggle with isolation, loneliness, frustration, weariness, and hopelessness. I searched through many books, but found they were written about how caregiving should go. Caregiving is not about how it should go, instead it is about creative problem-solving, resources, self-care, and walking smoother paths, leading you out into the light with your care recipient.

Caregiving is not for the faint of heart. You're lion-hearted--strong and looking for practical ways to excel as a caregiver while reading this book.

Inside these pages, you will find vulnerable real-life stories, helpful resources, and faith-based meditations for you to personalize. Detailed practical how-to's will guide you into the day-to-day of caregiving.

Two Roads

How I'd love to sit down with you by a cozy fireplace and listen to your story. I'd savor your words, every last thing you shared. We were like old friends reminiscing with each other about what we have been through: the struggles, the beauty, the loneliness, the hope, the losses. A road for fewer travelers.

> *"Two roads diverged in a wood, and I –*
> *I took the one less traveled by,*
> *And that has made all the difference."*[1]

---

1 A portion of The Road Not Taken, by Robert Frost, https://www.poetryfoundation.org/poems/44272/the-road-not-taken

We were coming from the same place of reference, you and I. We understood each other without saying a word. And when words came, our talk was deep, from the heart. We had tremendous courage to keep moving forward through our lives.

Protectors

We are Protectors. "A person or thing protecting someone or something. A person in charge of a kingdom during the minority, absence or incapacity of the sovereign." [2]

Advocates

We are Advocates. "A person who pleads on someone else's behalf."[3]

And there we are. It's what we do. It's part of who we are, now. We are there while we're watching others come and go, happily moving on with their lives. We are eagerly helping and at our wits end, all in the same day. Once in a while we get an unexpected, but grateful "Thank you!, while the next day our care recipient may be confused, angry, biting, swearing, or yelling.

We carry it all. Without Jesus Christ, the load is too much for anyone to bear alone. I would have quit on life a long time ago and missed out on such precious moments of living. Jesus has made all the difference for me. He will for you, too, if you let Him. Whichever road you choose, I'm here for you.

We're on a road less traveled, full of smooth asphalt,

2 https://www.lexico.com/en/definition/protector
3 https://www.lexico.com/en/definition/advocate

shifting gravel, bumps, dips, and deep potholes. The signs are down, so they take us by surprise. But once you know where the potholes are, the road becomes much smoother. Not easier, but smoother transitioning. Still, it's a road less traveled. And there may be a sinkhole or two. I can solidly tell you, it's all worth it. You are growing in courage and embarking on a daring adventure. I applaud you.

Rosalyn Carter said it first and she said it best:

"There are only four kinds of people in the world: those who have been caregivers, those who are currently caregivers, those who will be caregivers, and those who will need caregivers."[4]

Happy Penguins

Every single person will become a caregiver or care recipient. It may be for a day, a year, or decades. Some will embrace it, like we did. We've lived in the zoo. Others will only look at the happy penguins or fuzzy swimming polar bears. They allow others to go to the reptile cages alone. And some purely ignore it, even though the elephant is still sitting in the center of the room. They pretend not to see.

We are caregivers. Caregiving is life-changing. It can make you better or bitter.[5] The choice is up to you. Caregiving, if you decide to allow it, can create an intimate daily walking with God: redefining your values,

---

4 https://www.nextavenue.org/rosalynn-carter-pioneering-caregiving-advocate-says-more-must-be-done/
5 Partial quote by Peggy Roloff while swimming at LA Fitness with me, Hillsboro Oregon

reshaping your heart, and refocusing on what is most important to you in your life. There's no room for pride in caregiving. It's a humble walk. It's the only way you can do it.

A few of you happily walked into the complex land of caregiving with a positive mental attitude, bright hopes, and courage. However, many more were plopped down into the middle of caregiving, much like you plop down on the couch after a long day. Perhaps it was a group effort with siblings, or when lots were drawn, it all fell to you. I imagine you may be starting the caregiving journey; searching for answers, practical how-to resources, truth, and wisdom. I admire your great courage already; the first walk out into caregiving.

Brave hearts

You are a brave heart. Even if you are physically weak, the kind of strength you need has little to do with the body, but totally to do with your attitude, your strength of mind, your love, your relationship with Jesus Christ, and your forgiving, humble, and strong spirit.

You are never alone walking on this path. Follow God's lead. I've gone before you to lead the way. You have nothing to fear. There's only love ahead. Not the gushy, mushy kind of love. The deep, real love. The messy day kind of love. The rich love. The love few know or are brave enough to embrace. The sacrificial love. The love given us by Father God brings courage for each day, not the year ahead; courage for today, and it's enough.

5

You will develop an undaunting spirit as you are caregiving. Don't panic. You will become stronger. You will learn to care for yourself well. You will speak truth and life to yourself and others. Caregiving is not for the doubting, weak-minded. You are resolute and you are learning the art of caregiving. You are fearless and brave.

In Greek, character is defined: to chisel; engrave or carve; what's left after you've been gouged out. You will be growing in character in all the yet undeveloped areas. I'm so proud of you already.

At the end of each chapter, an interactive "Here & Now" section personally written for you, will feed your soul, encourage your heart, and strengthen your mind to keep you going forward.

Forty hands-on, detailed "Practical Tips" are listed in the Appendix in the back of this book, giving you step-by-step instructions to successfully accomplish each caregiving task with ease. I learned them the hard way, and am passing them all on to you.

Thank you for choosing my book. I am humbled. Turn the page and let's get started, Courageous One.

Here & Now Reflection

COURAGE

Courage is the quality guaranteeing all your other qualities. Courage to love. Courage to believe. Courage to follow Christ. When you are courageous, it is not puffing yourself up, looking as strong as iron. Real courage is a weighted blanket covered with humility, and a king-sized pillow of vulnerability.

No matter where you are and how little time, nurture yourself. You will never regret it. Read a few pages in a book. Go for a stroll. Sketch. Paint. Bird-watch. Plant a flower. Sit and soak in the sunshine. Learn a musical instrument. Listen to music you love. Sit in silence. Go to the beach. Bask in the presence of a close friend. You are taking care of yourself with kindness. You are exercising relentless courage.

When was the last time you were courageous?

In what way were you kind to yourself lately?

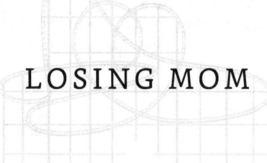

LOSING MOM

My mom, my five-year-old son, Jordan, and I sat alone in the doctor's waiting room. Mom was relaxed, and seemed oblivious to the gravity of the situation; I was three-straight-espressos tense. Just forty-eight hours earlier, my brother, Jim, called me in Maui. My husband and I were celebrating the sale of our coffee-roasting business and our early retirement with Jordan.

"Kay Nell, Mom fell, hit her head on the stove handle, and we took her to the hospital. She had a stroke. She's back home now but needs follow-up appointments."

Even though it didn't pass Jim's lips, I knew I was the one. I would be the caregiver.

On the painfully long flight from Maui to Portland, my mind raced.

Will she come back from this? Will she be permanently disabled? Will she need 24/7 care? What is the extent of her loss? Not only her loss, but mine. Do I have what it takes for the days ahead? For the possible years ahead? I just retired! I thought there were carefree days ahead!

Testing the Waters

At her age of eighty-three, and her third husband the age of ninety-two, I should have seen the tidal wave coming, but I wasn't looking for it.

I tried to casually assess Mom's mental state.

"Mom, what is two plus two?"

She scrunched up her face into a confused look, then confidently said, "Five."

"Good, Mom." I flashed an insincere smile. *Crap, that's haywire.*

"Humor me here, Mom. What is your name?"

"Ummm, well, you're Kay Nell and I'm your mother." *She didn't state her name at all. Weird.*

"Do you know what year it is, Mom?"

"Well, it's 1997." *One right.*

"What's your address?"

"Ummm, well…oh, you know where I live. I can't think of it right now."

Next, I handed her a book to read to her five-year-old grandson, Jordan, whom she adored. I used it to distract her. *Can she read?*

She was reading solidly to him at his kindergarten-level text. My heart lightened a bit.

"Kathryn?" the receptionist was apparently glued to her chair.

Mom was known as Kathryn as an adult: in her 1930s Bridgeport, Nebraska high school, she was known as Katie, Kat, M.K., and Shorty. My dad's loving name for her was Punk.

"Mom, that's us. Let's go."

She slowly, stiffly, rose and ambled her walker down the long, narrow hallway into the room a nurse pointed out.

"The doctor will be with you in a few minutes."

"Thank you." I had painted a smile on my face. I loved the doctor, as he was a preventative MD--not an alarmist--full of wisdom, and godly.

He came into the room and closed the door.

"Well, what happened here to you?"

Mom glared at him. "I'm fine. I don't know why I'm here!"

Yep. That's my mom. Confident.

"Mom, you had a stroke."

Now she glared at me. "I did not!"

I looked at the doctor, embarrassed my mom was talking so uncharacteristically. She was known for her kind, servant's heart.

"Yesterday she fell, hit her head on the stove handle and doesn't remember doing it. My brother and his wife came and took her to the hospital. She was out of there within a few hours and told to follow up with you." I stated the facts quietly, like the guy on the classic Dragnet TV show.

"She had a stroke."

"I did *not*! You keep your mouth shut!", she barked like a rabid dog.

Who is this woman?

I looked at the doctor again and shrugged my shoulders in resignation, so Mom couldn't see. He knows. I know. She had a stroke. She is not the same. He scheduled an MRI.

Inside the Tube

She could no longer drive, so the next day we stared at a huge, round machine in the middle of a hospital room.

The attendant pushed a button and Mom glided into the tight tube.

It may make her more comfortable if I stay in the room with her.

I slowly, gently massaged her feet until a loud voice echoed inside the tube.

"I think I could go to sleep if you'd quit messing with my feet!"

With fear and frustration, I rolled my eyes. *Oh, it's gonna be a bumpy ride.*

Another tidal wave hit at two o'clock in the afternoon the following day.

Sinking Sand

"The cortex of her brain is slowly dying off and there is nothing to stop it. She will slowly lose more and more of her memory."

Mom didn't appear to understand what the doctor said, nor did she care. He was compassionate with her as he explained vascular dementia in layman's terms.

What in the world?! What does this mean? Where are our lives heading? I've never been down this road. It feels like changes are happening at ninety miles per hour!

Outwardly, I appeared strong as an ox, who may be pulling a heavier load soon.

Mothers and Daughters

My thirteen-year journey with Mom began here.

Our mother-daughter vibe was usually warm and supportive, but there were days, as in any family.

"Are you going to wear those jeans with holes in them?" We had already left home.

"What size are you? I'll pay you to lose weight. I can't believe you're wearing such a large size. People who are little are so cute. Kendra and Jane are little and so cute!"

Bite me. I am not enough. I am too much. I will never be little and cute. What's wrong with me? Why am I unlovable the way I am? Why am I defective? Is she being mean and manifesting the effects of the stroke? I'm confused. I have no idea what's happening to her and to me. I feel so ashamed I'm not enough and too much simultaneously.

A tidal wave engulfed me there, standing in the sand, and I was sinking.

Just Me and Him

Mom's third husband was frantic.

"Kay Nell! You need to come here right away. I can't wake your mom up. Something is really wrong with her."

I walked into her room and she looked completely at rest.

Is she in a coma or is she dead? I've called out her name several times and there's no response.

"Mom, what's going on? Mom. Mom!" I shook her gently to try to awaken her. Her eyes remained closed as she spoke.

"Oh, Kay Nell, I don't want to come back. It's just too beautiful. It's the fulfillment of life. Complete resting. No more struggling. Weightless. I could hear my husband trying to get me up to eat breakfast, but I didn't want to come back. Food was so far removed and unimportant; I had no desire for it at all. I did not see any people or streets of gold. Only me in Jesus' presence, and that was everything. Personal. Just me and Him. You know the quiet time you have and think is so important, Kay Nell? Well, that's okay. Do that. Because that is all there is, living in the presence of Jesus. I did not want to wake up or come back at all. Kay Nell, I was looking for you. Be sure you are there in heaven. I did not miss anyone. None of that. Only me in the presence of Jesus, and that was everything."

Take the Journey

Through the years, many women told me how extremely proud my mom was of my brother and me, and how wonderfully we treated her. She said, "I love you" often to us and meant it deeply, as she did throughout our lives; but the many accolades from others didn't reach my ears until she was in the cold days of dementia with me. Their words soothed my soul.

Here we were today. Leaving a doctor appointment and I knew there would be more. I had no idea who she was in moments, where we were heading, how long we'd be traveling or who would go along with us. A trip we were going on together, but neither one of us wanted to take the journey. It may be for a long or short time. We didn't know. But we were going. Together. Regardless of other storms ahead.

Here & Now Reflection

LET GO

Let go. Do what is before you. You have divine appointments today. God has people for you to encourage, help. Maybe He's asking you to give a simple smile.

Let go. Focusing on the next carrot out ahead of you or looking back and wishing things were different is a waste of your brain cells. It assures you're missing out on today, this moment. Prepare for the days ahead as best you can. Don't live there in anticipation.

Let go. God's got this. He's not surprised. You're on the right path. One thing I know: He always shows up at the right place, at the right time. He's never late.

How will you prepare for situations you're facing?

How will you let go and welcome your divine appointments?

UNABLE TO RESIST

CHAPTER NAME HERE

CHANGING ROLES

The first time I changed roles with Mom was the day my dad died unexpectedly. She looked lost, with pools of water spilling out her brown eyes. It was then I started my four years taking care of her.

"Mom, would you like me to mow the lawn for you?"

"Mom, it's okay to cry. I'll hold you. You're going to be okay. You'll find your way."

"Yes, Mom, I can balance your checkbook for you and pay your bills."

"You want to come out to our place for dinner? I could pick you up and drive you home."

"You couldn't find your way home from Fred Meyer, but you found your way to Jim's home three miles away, and he took you back home. Good job, Mom."

Presenting well

Connie birthed her daughter one year earlier than my arrival. We all went to the same church. She opened a successful local fabric store and was a professional seamstress. She could fix any sewing mishaps in our county.

Decades later, she lived in the same assisted-living facility as my mom.

Her daughter helped me. "Mom presents well to people."

And she did. No one could tell she had Alzheimer's. Sometimes Connie and I played a game; a memory game.

I cozied up to her on the couch in front of a glowingly warm fireplace.

"Connie, you are an amazing woman. You've been so kind to people. You owned a fabric store in Forest Grove up on 21st and Main Street. You helped so many women with their sewing problems and needs. There's never been another fabric store like yours in town again."

She smiled.

"Connie, remember when your daughter and I were teens and I'd call to talk with her on the phone?"

Connie nodded.

"When I'd call, Morrie, your husband, would tell me his daughter wasn't there, but would I like to talk to his first wife? And the joke was you were his first and only wife!"

Connie chuckled and broadly smiled.

"He was constantly playing jokes with people on the phone! Do you remember when our house burned to the ground while we were at Mt. Hood? Morrie led the church clean-up team along with his Bobcat dirt-moving machine. This was a long time ago, as I was married only three years by that time. I was twenty-two years of age."

Connie wanted to remember, but she was content I was remembering for her. She was a blessing to me.

My dad went to heaven only three short months prior to our home burning to the ground. God provided more than enough when we were at our lowest. I was severely depressed over the death of Dad. It was my first major loss in life. Then God did what only God can do. He resurrected dead me, lifted my severe depression while I did heavy manual labor for months. Our home was rebuilt on the same foundation, and nine months later, we moved in with joyful hearts, deep gratitude and three Old English Sheepdogs.

Connie smiled often, for no apparent reason. She had been married to a man who made her laugh.

"I need to go upstairs to visit my mom now, Connie."

"Tell her hello for me."

"Absolutely."

I scooched off the couch to stand, and leaned over to hug her.

"I'll see you tomorrow, Connie!"

Are your parents changing in their health? Are you adapting to new roles in relationship to them? We change roles with parents as they age, at least in some ways, but they are still and always will be our parents. They may be saying and doing things like children; they are not. They deserve our respect, honor, mercy, forgiveness, grace, and love. These qualities are not dependent on parenting deficits with us in the past.

Show respect

Thoughtfulness and attentiveness are gifts to give your parents. Perhaps they were thoughtless and inattentive in your childhood, but you can show them these gifts and give them as a gift to your own spirit, too.

Show honor

Fulfill your obligation to your parents for raising you. They sent you out into the world, whether it was through abandoning you or launching you. Your integrity and honesty are a vital part of your obligation. Welcome it.

Show mercy

A good illustration is the story of the 37th President of the United States, Richard Milhouse Nixon (1969-1974). He had committed crimes; impeachment and removal from office was imminent. Instead of dragging the country through judicial proceedings, Nixon resigned. His Vice President, Gerald Ford, took office in 1974 and quickly gave Nixon a full, free, unconditional pardon. The pardon carried an accusation of guilt, and as he accepted, it carried a confession of guilt. In short, Ford showed mercy to Nixon.

Forgive

Forgive if you harbor resentment or rage toward past crimes against you. Forgiving is not dependent upon an apology. You need to be a free caregiver now. Do the forgiving work early into your new caregiving role. Peace will come rushing in, and the weight of unforgiveness will lift off.

Show grace

Find ways to extend kindness, not for anything your parents or others did or didn't do. Kindness always flows back towards you. It's the principle: what you put out into the world comes back to you tenfold. Show unmerited favor toward others.

Show love

Patience, kind deeds, and humility are your friends. Irritability and a resentful attitude will not serve you or your care recipient. Let love be your greatest aim.

Jesus Christ shows us respect, honor, mercy, forgiveness, grace, and love every day. Look for where He is working. It's wherever you are right now, there in front of you. Do you see it? Watch for His love in action. Choose to be His hands, His feet, and His voice.

Nearly Undetectable

Your care recipient may look and behave the same, but subtle changes may be under the surface. When dementia tapped gently on my mom's door, it was nearly undetectable. Others didn't see it. I saw it. It was in her eyes. My brother, Jim, saw it when she couldn't find her way home from a store, but she always found his country home to ask for help. She welcomed gentle helping. You will see it in your care recipient's eyes, if you dare to gaze. And I know you'll dare to gaze, because you're strong, confident, and welcome the art of caregiving.

Mom was a people person, with strong serving skills. My dad and mom were entrepreneurs in real estate for nearly thirty years. After my dad's passing and a year had flown by, Mom retired.

She walked two miles a day, encouraging housebound elderly. She finished combing the hair of one, walked farther down the road to feed another, and walked back home. Everyone loved her. I loved her, but my dad was "my person." His quiet, wise, and listening personality felt like home to me.

Mom called daily to download her day. Then she hung up. I was sensitive to her needs. I set my grief, my thoughts, and my needs aside and considered them unimportant. She didn't ask how I was doing, what my day was like or if I was busy. She downloaded what she had for breakfast, her schedule for the day, who she was helping or visiting, and how her new violin lessons and organ practicing were progressing.

In person, she cried on my shoulder often. I felt I needed to be strong for her, so I consoled, and stuffed my sad feelings down without a tear. With each call, I felt more alone and depleted emotionally. I began setting a precedent of not sharing my thoughts, feelings, and needs in my close friendships. Even today, I listened and asked questions with one. Another called to share their needs. When I hung up each time, I felt depleted. They were uninterested in my life and I allowed them to download their agenda. Once again, I was wondering how I draw those people up close into my life, and why I was defective, when that wasn't the question at all. Eventually I understood the phone calls were opportunities to pray with friends and on my own. The depleted and defective feelings walked out my door, and prayer quietly walked in.

Elderly teenagers

Four years after my dad died, Mom married Don and relief flooded me, with new freedom in tow. At sixty-seven years of age she had a new person to intimately interact with and bask in their new lives together. They visited our country home during their two-month dating spree. Don was friendly.

"Kay Nell, you have a really nice home here in the country." Mom giggled.

"What did you name your three dogs?" Mom giggled.

"Moe, Mary and Shirley, like the Stooges." Mom giggled.

"Those are clever names. My cat's name is Hey Cat. He sits in my workshop to be vacuumed by my Shop Vac instead of brushed." Mom giggled.

They left.

Who were those people?!

They married, shot wild turkeys, ocean fished, and traveled extensively. Their love and my freedom spanned a short three years. She was his faithful caregiver for several months, and she aged about ten years right in front of our eyes.

A few days after Don went ahead of her to heaven, I drove Mom to the store. She looked frail in the passenger seat of my cargo van. I drove around a corner too fast, and without her seatbelt fastened, she fell out of the seat towards me. I helped her back up. We giggled together how it was a metaphor of her life that day—nothing but God holding her. Her quick ways were waning with this second deep grief within seven years. It took some of her zippy feistiness everyone adored. Again, I didn't realize I was entering into a new level of caregiving with her.

Keep living

At seventy years Mom's eyes were sad, and weariness seeped through her body. Her tight relationship with God never waned, but grew deeper. Once again, our relationship was changing. She was back to debriefing her days to me while I was at our coffee roasting business. Eventually, Phil hired her for a warehouse position as a Coffee Flavoring Specialist. She loved working for Phil. He allowed her to come and go as she wished.

As an avid violinist, she performed with the Senior Serenaders musical troupe. One of her four sisters played the washboard. Mom busied herself with music, encouraging others, and over time became the Minister of Visitation for our church, visiting all the people who could no longer come to church or were in the hospital. She had a heart for people in need, and she loved this ministry.

Never too late

At a spry eighty-one years, a quick two-month romance, and she was marrying an active ninety years of age man. He adored her—Harry

"We're wanting to get married right away. Why wait? What do you think about it?"

She asked like she was placing a grocery order.

"Well, it seems kind of soon. You've only been dating a couple months, Mom."

"Oh yes, but we've known each other sixty years."

"True."

In the 1940s, before Mom had children of her own, they co-taught the Jr. High teens at church: she, the girls, and he, the boys.

"Well, I thought I'd ask you, but we're going to get married anyway."

"Okay. Let me know the wedding date. I'm all in with you."

The date was set and I called a local TV station. Their limousine and TV interviewing crew met them amidst birdseed tossing as they left the church. Their love story was on the six o'clock news. They were adorable.

"Limo driver, take us to our honeymoon at the coast!"

They moved into his sprawling home, set in a tree farm near the edge of town. Our family enjoyed a few holidays and celebrations in their home.

Mom aged two years and two months before experiencing her first stroke there, as I returned from Maui. The door swung open for me into caregiving: transporting to doctor appointments, bookkeeping, bill-paying, hair appointments, shopping, bandaging wounds, catheterizing, lab work, massages, changing diapers, and laundry duties. The door also opened to hours of listening to her thoughts, memories, and hopes.

When she asked me to go through her office desk, I

realized she was no longer the same tidy businesswoman. Her penmanship had changed, money donated had changed, and bookkeeping was in disarray. I saw it all and felt the bottom had dropped out of my world. This was not how I wanted to spend my early retirement. A letting-go was on my plate. I knew God was on the move. Even so, I did not let go easily, and it was not always pretty.

Harry's daughter arrived.

"Dad, I think you should move into an assisted-living facility. Your wife could go live with Kay Nell."

She left.

"Harry, we're married and not living separately. I'll go with you if they are insisting you move."

"Well, I don't want to leave you either. That's not what we wanted. Thanks for going with me."

Now I was going through my mom and Harry's winters. Phil and Jordan were bright lights in my days mixed in with the increasing caregiver responsibilities. We sowed laughter and went on short adventures. God, Phil, and Jordan were tethers in the tornadoes swirling around me in the emergency rooms, with dementia adding a twist to everything.

Very big deal

"There are guns here and people are shooting!"

"Are you sure, Mom?"

"Well, you jackass, you think I don't know what I'm talking about?!"

Did she call me a jackass? Mom never even said gosh, pregnant, darn, or any swear words. Who is this woman?

I raced into town with my emergency blinkers on and ran into her apartment. The TV was on a shoot 'em up western station.

"Oh, Mom, it's just a TV station; but I can see how it was upsetting and why you thought they were in your room. I'll put a note on the TV for the gals so it's always on HGTV. That's a happy channel you'll like. I'm glad I can be here for you."

"Oh, I hate to bother you."

"You're not bothering me. I'm happy to help. It's no big deal."

It was a very big deal. The adrenaline was pumping frequently. I was feeling torn in several directions. The calls were frequent. I bought her an extra-large numbered phone, with my brother and I on a one-button push for her. This made Mom as independent as possible. A peace washed over me when she could no longer dial the phone. Caregivers dialed for her. When she could no longer walk (non-ambulatory), I wasn't concerned about her getting lost. Those changes were devastating, even though it made my life technically easier—sadness was constantly in the background of my mind now.

Here & Now Reflection

TWENTY-FOUR HOURS

Live the next twenty-four hours. The next twenty-four hours of caregiving and living your life to the fullest. If you play an instrument, bring it with you to play. If you sing, go for it with your care recipient.

Go to your exercise class or workout alone, if it suits you better. Choose to move forward, even if it is the minutest step. Move forward each day and you will keep going. The road is not easy, but you chose it. I'm so proud of you and who you are becoming as a caregiver.

What do you feel most proud about as a caregiver up to this point?

What will you do to keep going forward and embrace the next twenty-four hours?

PUSHING FORWARD

"I think Harry died."

"I'm on my way, Mom."

Mom was eighty-six years and Harry (her third husband) was ninety-five. He was a kind, godly man. With the emergency flashers on my black '97 Eclipse Turbo, I sped to her assisted-living facility fourteen miles away.

I quickly stepped into her outside-entry apartment. She was quiet, looked small and numb, without tears, in the pink recliner I'd recently bought. It was a fact; her husband lay dead in their bedroom. I dialed his adult children, who lived locally and were in their sixth decade.

"Wait for the mortician. They should be there in an hour or so. We're not coming."

"Oh. Okay."

The voice on the other end of the line was cold. They were not coming. I was shocked.

"Mom, the mortician will be here in a bit. I'll handle everything. We'll just wait and then you can come out and spend the night with us."

"Yes, I'd like that, Kay Nell."

Keep pushing forward.

I respectfully covered him with a sheet and waited for the mortician's arrival. We waited together in the living room. The mortician arrived two hours later.

"I'm here to pick up Harry."

"He's in the bedroom."

They did what morticians quietly do. When they left, I slowly drove Mom to our home.

"Will you give his things back to his family for me?"

"Of course, Mom. No problem."

"I'd like them gone before I go back to my apartment."

"You're free to stay with us for longer, if you like."

"No, I'll go back tomorrow."

At this point, Mom could walk slowly, and dementia wasn't detectable this evening. At five in the morning, I drove back to Mom's apartment and started dismantling the bedroom of his possessions. Adrenaline was surging through my body as I stacked all his belongings by the entry door. I couldn't believe what I'd been doing the past eighteen hours. I wasn't only responsible for Mom, but finishing up what his family was responsible. I called his family at seven in the morning.

"Please pick up all of your dad's things from Mom's apartment. It's all in one place. She wants it gone before she returns. She needs to move forward."

"Oh. Okay. I guess we could do that."

Yeah, ya think?!

Want it badly

They overreached when they nabbed the only thing Harry's sister made Mom for their wedding day, a small needlepoint footstool. When I brought her back to the apartment, she noticed it was gone.

"Oh, well. If they want it badly, they can have it."

She had a forgiving spirit always.

At the accountant's office during the previous tax season, she learned his family cleaned out their shared bank account. The disrespect towards my mom was astounding. I was livid.

"Oh, well. If they want it badly, they can have it."

Her forgiving spirit again. She never held grudges. In time, I followed suit.

His family planned the funeral at our church, without consulting Mom about anything. I was bent on moving forward. She needed this in her rear-view mirror, and so did I.

I began doing for Mom what she could not; attending care meetings, appointments, playing easy card games, going on slow walks, and driving her to my home for meals.

Wandering around

One day, she ambled down the hall, past the receptionist, and out the sliding doors with her rolling walker, turned right, crossed elevated railroad tracks and down a little hill. A gal in her yard saw her.

"Hi, Kathryn! It's good to see you out and about. You look a little tired. Can I help?"

"I can't remember how to get back home. I'm lost."

"Oh, no problem. I know exactly where you live. Remember? You sold us our home decades ago. We're friends!"

The gal heaved the rolling walker, and wedged it into the trunk. They visited the quarter mile back to Mom's one-bedroom apartment.

When she was ambulatory, Mom was a busy one, with a light touch of dementia, and kept me on ballerina toes.

Dancing ballet

"Kay Nell, don't you think you'd like to take ballet? Lois is an excellent instructor, and I think you'd learn to be more graceful. You're kind of tom-boyish and you could walk more gracefully."

So, basically I'm a project now. At ten years old, I even knew it. I experienced deep rejection, humiliation, bullying, and shame during class, week after week. My ballet classmates were already dainty and cliquish; I was odd-girl out. I was ten-years old.

Once starting anything, our parents never allowed my brother and I to quit. It helped make me who I am today, plus a girl who dislikes ballet--except one night: I loved Ballet Folklórico de México while I was in México City. A ballerina's back zipper completely unzipped. Watching her try to gracefully dance her way off stage holding her costume was hysterical to my fifteen-year-old self. I laughed until I cried.

Humbling right hook

I've been many places where all I had left was to trust Jesus for each breath, each moment, each day. We often believe we control relationships, work, buying power, what others say, what others think, what others do and even how much they do or do not like us. We even start to think if we do caregiving correctly, tough things will not happen to us. It's an illusion.

Do you think you are all-powerful? Lest you think I'm pointing my finger at you, I believed I was extremely powerful some days, because I controlled my life and made fantastic things happen for myself (and others) by hard work. I thought I controlled my destiny one hundred percent. I had a personal relationship with God, trusted Him, and my business enjoyed tremendous momentum and I was grateful. To top it off, my son, Jordan, surpassed all my expectations, enriched my life, and so much more.

Eventually, we sold our business to an employee, and the bank CEO came by to welcome her. The CEO and I had a close relationship. She glided right past me and shook the new owner's hand. She didn't even give me a glance. I stepped back and realized my kingdom was usurped now. It was logical, but my ego took a humbling right hook.

Gratitude

Chefs, housekeepers, and nannies made my days easier while we worked long hours in the business. They were all indispensable, and I paid them generously. Ego took an uppercut after I retired and began scrubbing floors, processing laundry, and preparing meals. The best part was enjoying Jordan every single day.

"Ruth, what did you use to clean the floor and how in the world did you make it look so easy? What was the process you used to clean my house? It's a mess, now! Thank you for all the days I came home to a beautifully clean home, week after week, for so many years."

"Oh, Kay Nell, I was glad to do it."

"Leigh and Angie, how do you cook all the food for a meal and serve it piping hot without microwave use? I cannot believe how much you've done for me through the years. Thank you, thank you, for all the deliciously healthy meals you prepared for my family. You made cooking look easy, and cooking is not my forté."

"Marie and Angela, thank you for all the love you poured into little Jordan with such care. You listened to him and took him on many adventures. He loves you both. You made my life seamless. Thank you."

"Oh, he's such a sweet little guy. He was always so kind, and a pleasure to care for him. We miss him now!"

Always give words to your gratitude. Thank others for the great ways they have made you feel. Attitudes come in all shapes and sizes. Fear, guilt, blame, and shame are liars. Gratitude is the truth spoken from the heart.

Fear

Fear perceives danger, even when there is none, and always paralyzes.

Blame

Blame accuses others and distracts us from taking responsibility.

Shame

Shame is feeling flawed and defective within.

The days I allowed lies to permeate my thoughts, it was like I was riding my bike into a brick wall. When I silenced lies with God's truth, I was coasting downhill with the wind blowing in my hair.

All the difference

Through it all, my relationship with God was a constant. I knew the Truth of His Word and His rhema word (personal words to my spirit). He never left me, even when I struggled, wiggled, and tried to run away. God and I were still communicating. He heard me even though he didn't agree with me. As a caregiver, I was: confused, depressed devastated, enraged, encouraged, frightened, impatient, uninterested, overwhelmed, provoked, and apathetic.

I learned the perseverance of caregiving from my experiences. No one was there to teach me. I'd never walked this intensely emotional and difficult journey. I needed hiking boots, knee pads, a backpack, water, and walking sticks.

You have this book in your hands, so you'll know exactly where to walk and what to take for your own journey. You are a strong, brave caregiver, if you choose. You will know the truth of His Word and His personal word for you, too. And that will make all the difference.

Attitudes

Changing your thoughts changes your feelings and attitudes, which changes your actions and results. Any changes you make causes others to change, too. Oh, it may take time, but the paradigm will shift. What we speak goes out into the world and creates whatever we spoke and returns to us. Our words are powerful. God created the world saying, "Light!", and there was light. You are creating with every word you speak. Choosing good attitudes and truth-based words will change you and everyone around you.

You are human. Your attitudes will go up and down. Give yourself grace, in the same way you are giving grace to others every day. It's easier to give grace to others than to pour it out upon yourself. Grace is a gift you can give yourself right now, today. Jesus went to the Cross to give you grace, mercy, and abundant life today. Isn't it beautiful? You do not need to be "on" all the time for everyone. Walk in grace, mercy, and love, and everything will change; mainly, you.

Cool water

This is the worst day ever. I can't do this anymore. No one is helping! I'm exhausted. This sucks. No one is coming to save me. Nobody gives a rip.

I created repetitive thoughts. No grace, no mercy, no love, no problem-solving, no creativity, no hope, and no truth.

It doesn't matter what others are doing, I know I've been called to be a caregiver for Mom and I'm rocking it. I will have no regrets.

When I spoke truth, walked without fear, blame, or shame, I took responsibility and immediately experienced more grace, mercy, and love towards myself, and others. I was where God wanted me. I was still often alone and frustrated in caregiving, but He gave me generous hope and gentle life lessons to teach me. I decided to daily yield to Him and learn from Him without reservation.

What if your care recipient has a negative, judgmental attitude--ungrateful and it's driving you bonkers? You control your attitude, not theirs. Speak out love, grace, mercy, and truth to them. What gentle lessons is the Lord wanting to teach you through them? Maybe it's developing your character on a deeper level. Character is not sharpened in the blissful seasons of life. It's sharpened in the cutting of deep furrows and engraving seasons of persevering endurance. Allow God to take the lead in every season. His plans are good, even in the darkest of caregiving days, and your character will be growing deeper.

Stay watchful of your own attitude, not other's attitudes. Keep your thoughts, words, and attitudes aligning for good and they will spill onto your care recipient like cool water on a hot summer day.

Pouring compassion

Talk compassionately to yourself. I am highly compassionate toward others, but not as compassionate toward myself. How about you? A few years ago, I began making changes in how I treat myself. God's doing a work and I've made progress. I've been stubborn with Him sometimes. I'm in my sixth decade; some lessons have been long, difficult, and riddled with pain physically and emotionally. Pour a gallon of compassion upon yourself. You are pouring out. Fill back up.

Stop trying to please others and imagine what they are thinking. You have no idea what they are thinking, nor is it any of your business. Imagine they are cheering you on! Let it be enough you are speaking life to whomever is in your path today. If Jesus were there, what would He be saying to others, or to you? You usually will not know the impact your life-giving words have on others. Thoughts. Feelings. Attitudes. The only thing you have control over is your thought life today. Allow yourself to grow character and create a personal relationship with Jesus Christ through this awkward, exhausting, full-of-choices time as you are a caregiver, pouring out compassion like an endless stream upon yourself and those in your path.

Here & Now Reflection

HIS PRESENCE

I opened the door to my mom's apartment. Peace flooded me. His Presence. The Presence was always there. Thick. It was palpable. I wasn't surprised. Mom had an active, intimate relationship with Jesus Christ. Talking or not able to talk, the Presence of God permeated her apartment. The beauty in her room was holy, sacred. In her different-abilities, He was still with her--loving her and all who dared bravely to walk in, serving her with an open heart.

Are you currently experiencing fear, blame, or shame? If you need help untangling your thoughts, please seek help to work through them. You're worth it.

When was the last time you knew there was a flooding of His Presence?

What spiritual qualities have you experienced in your care recipient's space?

EMERGING
CHARACTER

The 1980s aerobic dance classes were my daily routine, along with colorful leotards, matching leg warmers, and headband. Jane Fonda's aerobic dances and floor workouts were the rage five days a week. Group circuit-weight training filled my hours after work twice a week.

Lifting weights and building a strong, muscular body takes time and commitment. So does caregiving. It flexes our muscles to grow stronger, think clearer, increase vitality, and persevere. A caregiver needs innovative ideas, refreshing moments, invigorating tasks, and encouraging words to renew. You will cultivate sustaining, nourishing good habits by creating new routines you pursue in your spirit, mind, and body.

You have perseverance. You haven't done anything yet? Yes, you did. You showed up. You are reading this book, telling me you want to be an exceptional caregiver, not mediocre. You want successful moments. You want to know how to do tasks efficiently. You have heart.

Kicking and screaming

Are you parenting your parents? Did you sign up for the job? Did a sibling or spouse sign you up? Do you think you are able to do the tasks? Will you find the time and stamina to be a caregiver? Is the care recipient's personality kind, angry, or somewhere in between? Are you a caregiver for a different-ability or chronically ill person? Are you the support person for another caregiver? Are you working at a facility as one of several paid caregivers? Were you thrown into caregiving kicking and screaming, or jumped in excitedly with both feet? I went in kicking and screaming inside my head.

Whether you embrace caregiving or kick and scream frequently, you and I are walking similar paths. We are caregivers. I've been embraced by it, enraged by it, confused by it, shocked by it, feared by it, dumbfounded by it, and cried my eyes out about it. I was called to be a caregiver for my mom. Deep in my gut, I knew it's what God wanted for me in this season of life, too. I knew I wanted to be there for her.

What's the big difference between caregiving and care doing?

Care doing

"I can do it faster and more efficiently; move aside. Here, let me do it for you. You're too slow! You can't do much for yourself without me. Give it here. I can't bear to see you struggling so much."

Those may be said verbally, with body language, or in your mind. Either way, care doing is about you and your agenda, your convenience, and your comfort level.

I arrived at the assisted-living facility irritated from the previous hours of my day. Mom was on a two-hour check. The caregivers logged in the date, time, tasks performed, and their initials in the notebook. A paid caregiver had not checked on my mom all night, but logged in about five-thirty in the morning, writing every two-hour check she did that night. She didn't do any of them. No one was in my mom's room for ten hours.

Mom's room video clearly showed my suspicions. The caregiver was falsifying records with every stroke of her pen. When I realized it, I thought, "Heads are gonna roll, baby." I was pumped up for the challenge. The Administrator knew a video camera was in Mom's room.

I walked long, fast strides to the Administrator's office.

I presented in a logical, calm manner, while my inner emotions were raging. I expected her to push me back verbally. She did not. Immediately, the paid caregiver was fired. I was surprised, but appreciated the integrity of the Administrator, and gained a deeper respect for the facility doing the necessary hard things.

Like a NASCAR driver, I've drifted around a few tough corners into care doing.

"Hurry up. I'm late!"

I can't believe how slow you are and now you want to talk more and you're not making any sense. I can't stand this. It's driving me batty. And now you didn't even thank me. I have a family and child responsibilities. A family I want time to enjoy. I was supposed to be there hours ago.

I didn't verbalize all my thoughts, but my body language showed. Sound familiar?

Caregiving tightrope

Caregiving says, "You're doing so well; the pace doesn't matter; it's that you're doing it."

Caregiving is the art of knowing how far to inspire and push into independence, and when to assist your care recipient. It's a tightrope. Find the balance and walk on it. Their ability may change tomorrow and they may be able to do more--or perhaps less. You are there to make your parent's life a more positive, encouraging experience while they are often living under tremendous stress, less mental capacity, and physically slower. May you decide to live intentionally today. Be gentle with yourself. Be gentle with them. Courageous One, grace yourself with kindness and gentleness today.

"Would you like me to help you with that or would you like to do it yourself?"

"I think you can do it yourself. Let me know if you'd like help."

"You're so smart, I bet you can figure it out."

"Would you like to wear this item or that item? Or do you want me to choose?"

Giving options increases independence, self-esteem, autonomy, and value. Today I drove her to hair and nail appointments. I closed the gates on a new boundary, doing for her what she can do for herself. She was walking up the ramp holding onto the rail. Usually, I'm right at her side, holding her arm. She spent about three minutes trying to stand up from the car. She preferred no help, so I was pleasantly waiting, instead of rushing to her side. Today she enjoyed more independence and self-esteem. I'm still learning.

You are eager to help your care recipient succeed, make choices, and do for themselves. You fill the rest in with your caregiving. Often, they have lost the ability to make choices between several things, and barely make any choices during the day. Facility-paid caregivers are on a tight schedule, often due to turnover and under-staffing. Creating independence for them is time-con-suming and exercises patience.

Are you doing too much care doing, thinking about your convenience, your comfort level, your endless needs? Maybe you are already doing a spectacular job caregiv-ing. If not, caregiving is waiting for you over there.

On your best days, you will feel a rhythm of ebb and flow with the care recipient's life; watching closely what they are capable of accomplishing on their own and what they are not. Remember, do not set them up to completely fail in a task. As you would a small child, encourage.

Building character

Which comes naturally to you? Care doing or caregiv-ing? No judgment, only an awareness. Decide which area will inspire creativity, problem solving, and true character growth in you. Be audacious and bold. Never shrink back. Embrace and acknowledge you are doing what most will not. Decide to completely succumb to caregiving and the emerging character growth God wants to work in you. God is smiling at you. You are truly fearless and patient. I'm so proud of you. He is, too.

"Take delight in the LORD, and He will give you your heart's desires. Commit your way to the LORD; trust in Him, and He will act, making your righteousness shine like the dawn."
PSALM 37:4-5 (CSB)

Here & Now Reflection

RELAX

Take an hour or longer and relax, close your eyes and listen. What do you hear in your spirit? The world will not stop turning if you take time for yourself. Take the time you need to restore. You are valuable. Renew yourself.

Describe how you become overwhelmed and exhausted while caregiving and the needs calling your name. What is the story you are repeating to yourself during these times? Perhaps you will need to rewrite your story to encourage yourself during the tough moments.

What encouraging word do you need today? Speak it over yourself.

What encouraging word are you willing to say to someone in your path today?

Who were you before you were called a caregiver?

Who was your care recipient before they needed a caregiver?

MOVING
BOUNDARIES

"Kay Nell, come pick me up, now!"

Mom called at six-thirty in the morning from her assisted-living facility.

"Why?"

"I need you to come get me right now. I've had it with Harry. Come and get me now!"

"I'll go pick her up for you." My husband, Phil, generously offered.

She's finally ready to come live with us and has had enough. They had a tussle a few days ago. She can go with me on Jordan's school field trip today. She loves to ride in the car.

"Mom, why didn't you pack anything to stay here?

"Oh, I need a day away. I'm going back."

You've got to be freaking kidding me! At six-thirty in the morning she's demanding we pick her up immediately and she didn't view it as a crisis situation at all. I'm emotionally exhausted already. I've been planning how to rearrange our home for her to live with us!

On the field trip my energy was sapped by her repetitive husband stories.

"Please wait at the back door here while I put some things in the car. I'll come back and help you down the steps, Mom."

As I hurry back from the car, Mom is halfway down the steps, bent at a forty-five degree angle, ready to somersault.

"Mom, I asked you to wait for me! I don't want you to fall. Here. Grab my arm and I'll help you one-by-one down the steps."

Asking too much

About halfway to her apartment, she leaked a few tears.

"Please don't be angry with me."

I've seen these tears before. It was hard for me, since I was always told to "Hush it up!" when I cried as a child. My tears embarrassed me even as an adult.

"Mom, you know I love you very much. You expect me to take care of all your appointments, business, make your life run smoothly, and listen to your marital problems that you're not willing to do anything about. Call your granddaughter, Heather. She's a good listener. You didn't raise me with marital conflict in the home. Truthfully, I have no idea how to handle all the things you tell me. I see things as black and white. I know you do not. You aren't doing what I would do and it's okay. But it sucks the life right out of me to hear about all your marital problems. I cannot do it anymore."

"I know, Kay Nell. I love you, too."

Respecting boundaries

I love my extended family. My brother, Jim, and mom didn't have problems with boundaries. Jim kept specific boundaries with her. He didn't listen to her marital issues and didn't visit her every day. He was dealing with early onset Parkinson's disease, sprayed with Agent Orange in Vietnam by his country. His plate was overflowing.

Boundaries can give life balance. They can also shelter, stifle, and self-protect you. You may find boundaries useful in your caregiver/care recipient relationship.

One healthy caregiving boundary for me was to finish caregiving before Jordan's school day was over. Did it happen one hundred percent of the time? Nope. Many times, he went with me as I gave care to Mom. Her bed was in the living room of her one-bedroom apartment where she saw birds fluttering, enjoyed sunlight, and listened and watched me play piano.

The beauty of boundaries is they are a gate to open, inviting others closer, or maybe next time closing the gate to create space, quiet, renewal, and solitude for yourself. Swing the gate open wide or shut the gate and lock it. It's always your choice to make.

Healthy boundaries

Boundaries create health and wellness in your life, not a goal of pleasing everyone. You will be the least happy not exercising boundaries and allowing others to routinely walk all over your life. Creating boundaries often brings conflict. However, the conflict it may create in the short term, is nothing compared to the chaos ensuing in the future, if boundaries are not set, and you are at the whim of others.

"No, Kay Nell, I don't plan to abide by what you need from me with my own grandson when he stays here for an hour."

"Well, that makes me incredibly sad, Mom. Since you made that decision, I'll need to make some decisions as a result. I'll see you later. Enjoy the rest of your day. Thanks for taking care of him today. I love you."

"I love you, too."

It was crystal-clear she didn't respect my boundary. It was a somber day as I realized the depth of refusal in accepting a simple boundary. Mom carried silently the brokenness of severe childhood physical abuse by an older brother from her age of five- to ten-years old. Gratefully, she did not carry any abuse forward into our family life. But it did come out in an absence of boundaries, an absence of crying, and an absence of empathy. She was godly, full of God's Spirit, a servant at heart, and a fantastic Mom ninety-nine percent of the time. We were fortunate.

Caregiving requires boundaries. You are Herculean in your caregiving, and your time has become more valuable. Create a few boundaries and stick to them. Not rigidly. You are worthy of any boundary you set in your life. Boundaries are not selfish. They bring balance, joy, calm, renewal, kindness, peace, and solitude.

Start with a simple boundary. When I awoke today, I stretched my body, sat a couple minutes, got my herbal tea, and grabbed my Bible. I read until a scripture jumped out from the page for me and then applied it to my day. I didn't reach for my phone. That's my boundary as of late. Does it happen every single day? Nope. I don't go for perfection, but moving forward as best I can.

There are time boundaries: What days will you be a caregiver? What time do you need for yourself? There are task boundaries: Will you do the tasks? Will you delegate the task to someone else?

Teaching moment

Will you go the extra mile? Will you pull up your sleeves and teach another caregiver how to help your care recipient so you can grab extra time for yourself? Teaching a substitute paid caregiver how to become a better one is good use of your time. Even though they are paid as a caregiver, it doesn't mean they know the nuances of your care recipient. Recently, I taught a caregiver how to use a hoyer (a lift for someone who is non-ambulatory). It's a common piece of caregiving equipment, but even personnel in large hospitals often have no idea how to use them. That's okay. It can be a teaching moment for you to humbly give them.

Allow time

Mom had a strong sanguine/choleric personality, She was highly results oriented and needed mega social time. I have a strong choleric/sanguine personality; strongly results oriented with limited social time. She often happily chattered. Her life was an open book. My life was under lock and key. I shared things with her carefully.

It made me depressed often when I was a teenager in angst, but at forty-five years of age, many others honored my privacy. I no longer kept knocking on the same door. No one was home there. God was faithful to each of us, even if sometimes we were not.

You don't need to do anything earth-shattering when you allow time for yourself. You might sit there staring into space, or you might do something creative, feeding your spirit; your choice. Make it your own. You don't have to be anyone for me. I already respect you. You are an adventurous caregiver. You know what you need already.

Stealing regrets

It takes practice to set up boundaries. Caregiving boundaries are foggier to me, because I want to do such a good job and give it my all. When the giving is too much and I have nothing left of myself, setting boundaries is yelling at me.

"STOP!" She yelled from the passenger seat of my car.

"What?! What's wrong, Mom?"

"Why don't you go over there and grab me a couple pieces of corn in that field? They'll never miss it."

Did I hear her right? Yep. I did. She was asking me to steal her a couple ears of corn.

"I can't do that! It's not ours. That's stealing from a farmer." I stated in my best Mom voice.

"Oh, come on. You can park there and go over and grab a couple. That's not stealing. What's wrong with you?" She was using her best persuasive Mom voice.

Another shaming lesson, but I was not dissuaded.

"No, I'm not stealing corn for you. We can go buy some from a farm."

Today I live across from a farm with endless cornfields. In my imagination, I change the outcome by pretending I stopped and picked her a couple corn ears. A grin spreads across her face as she touches the corn.

Regrets. I've had a few.

Here & Now Reflection

OPEN-WINDOW DAY

At six in the morning, I climbed out of bed, opened the large window and inhaled the crisp, clean morning air. I love open windows; the breeze blowing lightly into my home, a misty warm rain and fresh air permeates my senses.

Six years into my mom's slow-progressing dementia, she was having sporadic windows of lucidity. It had been about one week since she spoke to me in words.

This was an open-window day.

"Kay Nell, I love you more than you know."

I'd forgotten the last time she initiated a deep, personal thought. Nearly every day of my growing-up years, she'd fling out a sincere, heartfelt "I love you!" to my brother and I.

But this day when she spoke, it was like fresh, warm rain pouring over my spirit from the hand of God. It's the little things in life.

The "I love you more than you'll know" moments.

Watch for them. Create them for others you love. Bask in the open windows of living.

When was the last time you felt a priceless moment, even if it was in a joyful or sorrowful time?

_____

_____

Who could you say, "I love you more than you know" to today?

_____

_____

What boundary needs to be adjusted in your life?

_____

_____

CHANGING
DIRECTIONS

My heart sank when I heard the name of the nursing home Jordan's second-grade class was going to for
Valentine-Sharing Day. I'd been hoping for maybe one
of the retirement homes, something with fewer odors.
However, the kids never made a peep. They happily put
their coats on, Valentine cards in hand, and chattered
about their class party that I'd planned for later in the
day at his private Christian school.

Most of the girls were walking quietly to the double
sliding doors of the nursing home, while my carload of
eight boys plopped their feet in every mud puddle between
the car door and where the girls patiently waited. I sauntered inside behind them, pretending to slowly herd them
in the right direction. My feet were dragging, mimicking
my dragging thoughts about the luck of the draw that
morning. The performance room was at the end of the
center hall and the kids filed in willingly. They slowly
walked around the room, gently handing the Valentine
cards they made to people in chairs, wheelchairs, and
beds. Many residents were unable to respond, but that

didn't stop the second-graders. Even the shy ones gave their Valentine cards away easily.

It's all about me

Reluctantly, I made my way down the hall, positioned myself outside the door so I could see Jordan sing, but not make eye contact with anyone else. You'd think I'd never gone to a nursing home. On the contrary, I spent many of my first eighteen years following my mom into nursing homes, played the piano for residents, recited Bible verses, served communion, and anything else my mom was sure I could do. She spent countless hours caring for the elderly and brightening their days. This day Mom would not be proud of me. I wasn't proud of me. I didn't force myself to levels of discomfort.

Wasn't I doing my part by driving the kids there and coordinating the party afterwards? Wasn't that enough?

I knew the answer, but pretended the answer was different.

Yes, that is enough.

She wheeled up slowly from about thirty feet away. I saw her young, smiling, contorted face staring through me. Glancing around, I was sure she must be heading somewhere else; I continued to intensely watch Jordan singing with his classmates. I saw her out of the corner of my eye, steadily working her wheelchair closer and closer to me. I took a step forward to not inhibit her direction.

She changed the direction of her wheelchair, came right up to my feet and stopped. Sweat was seeping through my skin to my cold, clammy hands. All this time, a smile was pasted on my face, by sheer determination.

What was she going to do? What did she want? Why is she here in front of me? What's she planning to do to me? Does she think she knows me? What do I say to her? How can I communicate with her?

She sat in front of me groaning words I couldn't understand and spastically moved her arms around at me. Her neon-red sweatshirt was seen from anywhere, next to her dark brown pants on her short, disfigured legs. Interestingly, her hair was cut much the same as mine--a long Dorothy Hammill cut, like the professional ice skater--except her hair was blonder than my salon-colored dark brown hair.

She wanted my hand. I knew it and so did the other moms who stood about three-feet away from me watching their children, but interested in what was going on between the neon-red sweatshirt and me. My head was spinning, but as she reached her arm out in spasms, she caught my hand in hers. My face flooded with heat. I was embarrassed by the attention, yet sweating in my armpits by now because of the unknown of what she would do.

Would she bite me?

My mom had tried biting me recently in a strong night of dementia. The red sweatshirt arm was dragging my hand upward towards her mouth.

Oh dear, what in the world is she going to do?

Character growing

She had quite a good grip, as my arm gently pulled back from her, afraid where this encounter was leading. The adult in me didn't want to make a scene in front of the mom peers, so the smile was still glued to my face. As she pulled my hand closer and closer to her mouth, I cringed inside. Time stood still. I no longer heard the children singing, but their mouths were moving. At the last minute, she turned my hand over with the back of my hand nearest to her mouth. She proceeded, ever so gently, to lightly kiss the back of my hand, while constantly gazing up at me with her large, blue eyes.

I moaned and with tears in my eyes said, "Thank you. You are very, very kind. You're very sweet. Thank you."

She slowly released my hand, crookedly smiled, and wheeled away.

I gestured my head towards the mystery girl at a nearby paid caregiver.

"What's her name?"

"Gloria."

Gloria humbled me from her old-as-a-shoe wheelchair, neon red sweatshirt and a haircut like my own. I felt small and foolish for holding my hand back from her, for not greeting her first and thinking of myself instead of young Gloria in the nursing home. Later, God brought me to my knees for my shallowness of heart, my ineptness at showing compassion.

Somehow, Gloria is still with me, teaching me at odd times to be humble, compassionate and fearless. It could be me in the wheelchair: disfigured, with spasticity, wearing a neon-red sweatshirt.

Preach it

Preaching was in Pastor Dale's DNA. Each day he arose early to read his Bible and pray intensely for his flock. Wednesday nights he led in-depth Bible Studies for the youngest to the eldest. He preached with fervor and knew the Word by heart. He listened and prayed with all. Empathy and love overflowed consistently from his mouth. He loved his wife and family profoundly.

His wife had passed and as an elderly, retired preacher with dementia slowly progressing, his daughter welcomed him into her home. In her living room stood a four-foot tall mahogany buffet, with framed photos expanding the length of it. The majority of photos were his sons, daughters and grandchildren.

Pastor Dale picked up one of the framed photos and he instantly preached, prophesied, prayed and encouraged the person in the photo. One by one he worked his way down the buffet daily. Some days he held Bible Study with them all. The legacy he is leaving, even as dementia overtakes him, is astounding to witness and priceless. It's really no surprise. After all, preaching is in Pastor Dale's blood and His Name will be the last thing on his lips.

Pastor Dale and Gloria were vulnerable and courageous. Courage requires vulnerability. Be fearless. What will be the last thing on your lips?

Here & Now Reflection

WEEPING

Weeping can indicate your great love for another. Healing is on its way to you in the midst of your weeping. Tears may say you are ready to accept healing. Let the tears flow. Never apologize for them. I apologized for every tear for years.

Now in my sixth decade, I let them flow unabashedly without apology. I love deeply. What an honor and joy to overflow with love. Perhaps your tears are nearby and waiting to heal your brokenness. Be gentle and kind with yourself. You loved deep.

Who do you love deeply?

_____

_____

What are the qualities you loved the most?

_____

_____

How could you apply one of those qualities into your life?

_____

_____

What character trait are you growing in lately?

WALKING PATHS

Fear permeated my mind, body, and spirit today. I found several nodules on my beloved six-year-old Old English sheepdog, Norm. I knew it wasn't good as I called his veterinarian. I cannot imagine living without Norm. My faithful companion. I never had to look for him. He was always by my side. Fear paralyzed me. A new rhythm is in view, and I don't like it.

It's an emotional thought common to the human race. Good fear keeps us from running out into the middle of a busy street. We've all experienced fear: the pounding heart, the sweaty palms, the anxiety. We call fear by other names. Chaos. Panic. Depression. Frustration. Worry. Overwhelmed. Confused. Scared. What if's. New rhythms conjure up all sorts of thoughts and emotions in our lives.

Fear

What is your latest new thing pressing you? Does it scare you? Or are you sensing you've got this? Whether your new thing is like a slow waltz, hard rock, bluesy, or drumming; it's new to you and an area to negotiate through. You are learning. You'll find the edge. Sometimes you may lose your way. The fear, panic, and worry set in. Sift through your thoughts. Negotiate your way through and out to your own new path. Take heart; you may even find joy in your new rhythm as a caregiver.

Make room

You think all you've heard about this caregiving sounds pretty good, a matter of organizing. And then you look at your own situation. Married? Single? Single parent? Little ones? Teens? Working at home or out? Empty nest? It can be a noisy, chaotic rhythm to juggle career, family, and add in caregiving for your care recipient. A new rhythm, a new territory, a new path to practice the unshrinking courage of caregiving.

You, as a caregiver, need to create a completely new set of rhythms. The rhythm of making room. You are consciously or unconsciously making room for your care recipient and all the people in their life and yours. It's good to make room. To scoot over for minor or major life changes.

Letting go

You may need to set aside your plans, your desires, your dreams to make room for your care recipient. There's no way to continue your life as you knew it and not let go. Others will tell you it is possible. But it will make you crazy to try to live it out. I know. I did it for a while. Thinking I could have it all, do it all, and juggle it all.

Breathe. Let go. Be bold and fearless. Set your own pace. Something will have to change for a time. Please do not let go of your self-care. It is not selfish when you make room to include yourself, as well.

Procrastinating

Caregiving resources are found everywhere; YouTube, Internet searches, nurses, mentors, audiobooks, etc. Analyzing and researching is great. However, you may fall into procrastination because you're not confident to take the next step and it's a bit overwhelming to gather information. Bottomline--listen to your heart, your gut, your brain. You know what is right. You know the next step. You know what needs to happen.

You know you are negotiating the art of caregiving perfectly when you realize there's no right way; but there is your way. And there's the right way of caregiving for you and your care recipient. It's of no consequence what others think. After all, caregiving may not be on their plate, currently. Rest assured, it will cross their path again on their life journey as a caregiver or care recipient. Never allow procrastination to be in charge. Research. Analyze. Pray. Make a decision.

Control

The NBA play-off tickets go for about $1,000-$2,000 each. The venue is a packed house, and when the game is over, throngs rub, shove, and push each other towards the exits. The crowd is massive. The only thing you can do is ride the wave to the next exit.

Have you been driving your way forward while you're caregiving? Are you rubbing, shoving, and pushing your way through? This may create feelings of anxiety, chaos, confusion; your feet on moving ground. I assure you, if you are caregiving, God sees and is in control. He has fully equipped you for caregiving and it is a good work you do. You are humbly in control as you seek Him each day. You are already in control, so there's no need to drive, rub, shove, or push your way forward today. Just ride the wave to the next exit.

Watchers

There are people who enjoy control for the sake of controlling others. Then there are people like you and me. You are comfortable--or learned to be--making decisions, without blaming others. You're at peace with the loneliness in caregiving. Others will be critical of your decisions. However, it's often the ones talking about caregiving as a concept, but never actually stepping into caregiving. They are able to resist and for humor and reality, let's call them "Watchers" for now. Please don't write Watchers off or cut them out of your life. You will desire it. They may blame, criticize, advise, and whine. They are watching you unable to resist, doing what they chose to avoid at this point in their lives. Watchers may regret it later, but that's none of your business.

Their path is not your path. Remember? You chose vulnerability, courage, and caregiving. They may be great resource people for making phone calls, bringing flowers/plants, birdfeeders, or even cooking a meal.

Moments may come, while you're in the throes of intense caregiving, when you need to keep Watchers at bay. They will slow you down and distract you. Your mind is sharp and on caregiving, problem solving, teaching, advocating, and connecting with your care recipient. There's no time for negativity or judging input at this point. Your plate is full right now.

"Hold the thought. I'll get back to you in a few days." Perfectly fine to say. Exercise the muscle now. Let the Watchers...watch. In their watching, you are teaching them by your actions, without words. What a privilege and responsibility you exert. Never listen to Watchers opinions about your caregiving. The only one to please is God.

Expectations

What are your best expectations in caregiving right now? Experience it. Imagine it. Set a small goal each day, a direction to head. Consistent, tiny goals will lead you to accomplishing your major goals, with your care recipient and in your life. Expectations can be perfectionistic, or absolutely no expectations in order to avoid disappointment. Expectations, if they involve your own behavior, are great motivating factors.

To outsiders, you make caregiving look easy and seamless. Watchers have no idea what caregiving entails. What can you accomplish today? Then do it. You don't need perfection. You need progress and pride about how you are a caregiver. Is your care recipient clean? Medications regulated? Comfortable? Safe? Then you had a fantastic day as a caregiver.

Notice I did not ask you if your care recipient was happy. It's not your piece of the caregiving puzzle. If happy, consider it an exceptional day. It's a decision the care recipient made, whether consciously or unconsciously. You did a fantastic job today! Kudos to you! You rocked it!

Seasons

This is a season in your life, the caregiver season. If I'd known how long it was, I could have prepared myself for the long haul. I went from one emergency to a brief reprieve and then another emergency. What I see in my rearview mirror now, I'm hoping you will learn from my experience; look through binoculars to see the overall view. Whether it's thirteen years, one year, days, months, or the rest of your life; this is your life. It's a season. Sometimes it will be spring or summer, and other times you will see fall coming and a dark, cold winter blowing in. Eventually, the season will end.

Whatever the season, try to rest--not panic--in the season you, your family, and your care recipient experience. There will always be pathways in your life to negotiate. Enjoy the process. Did you hear me? Enjoy the process, no matter what the season. I write that with the ease of my computer in the early morning entering into a beautifully sunny 101° day. I don't like heat, but prefer 60°. Enjoying various seasons will take focus. Wherever life finds you, this too shall pass. Savor moments. Welcome the ups, the downs, and the in between, with a loaded dose of hope.

Routines

Routines can bring you peace or make you suffocate. I've fluctuated from one end to the other. A sense of routine will definitely help you in the art of caregiving in an easy, gentle way. Rigid is not a routine. It's a ritual. There's a fine line between rigid and a good routine that makes your life easier, unencumbered by burdens you were not meant to carry. Make a point to be flexible. After all, caregiving is unpredictable at its best.

Create good ritual routines. Your spiritual growth is a great place to start. As you change your thoughts and your identity to line up with God's truths, your body will respond to the life-giving direction. If you're starting out, perhaps read in the Bible; the book of Acts, James or First John. Meditating and moving your body creates energy, and energy gets you into the flow of intentional living. Find a verse that catches your eye, think about what it means, pour out your heart to God, then apply it in your life that day. If you don't apply it, you will be religious; but the goal is a personal relationship with God through Jesus Christ. He already sees you through Jesus Christ and his accomplished work on the Cross. He loves it when we turn towards Him.

Decide what you need to include in your day to create a sense of wellbeing. If you believe you can keep your normal schedule and be a caregiver, you will resent caregiving and possibly the care recipient. You have overloaded your schedule. You resisted caregiving because it's not your gift. It's not where you feel the most alive. So what!

Caregiving is knocking on your door asking you to change your routines, your schedule, your desires, and yes, even the things you love. It's tempting to ignore the knocking. What you may truly be ignoring is the opportunity to grow deeper in your walk with God. The more we keep a tight grip and refuse to reach out for the new, we stifle our growth. Lest you think I created wellbeing every single day of caregiving...nay, nay. The days I started reading God's word, applying it, and moving my body in a fun way, my well-being greatly improved and I was better able to endure as a caregiver. When I no longer fought caregiving, the routines were easier and I found joy in the mundane routines of living.

There's another way to go into caregiving, too: delegating.

"Who may I get to do this task?"

Don't try to use guilt when asking someone. If they say, "no," use another resource. Remember you're using creativity in the art of caregiving. You're not roping others in as you delegate. If you are turned down, move forward to your next resource.. It's not surviving as a caregiver, but thriving and flourishing as you give care. Create a gentle, easy routine, and you'll negotiate the demanding days easier as a caregiver. Develop routines that welcome inner peace.

Research options

You could hire from a caregiving company already established. If you choose this path, realize you will be paying twice the amount of a professional caregiver, as the paid caregiver will receive a small portion, and the company will take the majority of the hourly wage. For me, a better way was looking to my sphere of influence and watching for those who would be excellent at caregiving. Maybe include student nurses, occupational therapists or physical therapists from a local college, or an extended family member. If you have parts of caregiving you would rather hire someone to do, do it! Don't agonize over it. You cannot be all things to all people. Your care recipient may not be happy when you hire anyone to help. Do it anyway; you're strong, you know yourself, and you want to negotiate forward, not scribble your way through. My experience was that the care recipient will adapt and see the benefits eventually. You will be more joyful and able to do other caregiving tasks with a more pleasant attitude and smooth pace.

Money

You may think you don't have enough money to hire someone. Think again. It's a matter of gathering resources. Perhaps family members will donate money. You might set up a crowd-sourcing page and tell your story. Hold out on buying everything on the planet. Sell items to generate cash. There are unlimited problem-solving ideas to help your care recipient and you succeed. Pursue every lead, and you will find resources and options. Open your mind. Don't get stuck in excuses. Don't try to make the care recipient's entire family happy. It won't happen. Be at peace with it. Take no personal offense.

Paths to walk

In my thirties I jogged two miles a day. I started by walking to a telephone pole and jogging to the next one over and over again until I jogged the entire two miles consistently. This took about ten weeks. Consistency was key. What path are you walking today? Keep at it.

Why did I ever think this was hard?

It will go through your mind at some point. Smile. Take it in. You gained an understanding of what it takes to be a caregiver. You not only understand it, you accepted it as part of your lifestyle. The knowledge you learned is serving you well.

Breathe in deeply who you are now. Today. Exhale slowly and know you will have no regrets, but only peace in what you are choosing to do with your life. You are doing the hard thing. You are not running from caregiving. You are embracing it, welcoming it like an old friend. Beautiful. Well done.

Take a break once in a while. Stay in your pajamas all day. Shower late. Snooze. My favorite nap happened reading a book with a little warm sun coming gently through the window, getting drowsy and drifting off to sleep. I've come to decide napping is an art. I can rarely make myself take a nap, and when I lay down to do so, my mind starts firing one hundred miles per hour. I have the fear of missing out.

My husband, Phil, catnapped easily and was out like a light. My eyes were wide open as I watched him nap. Whatever you choose, relax and breathe deep slowly. You are resting and it is good.

My favorite path to walk was on soft and squishy blacktop. Concrete jammed my knees and feet. It had no give to it. Sand gave with the weight of my body, pushed up between my toes and naturally exfoliated and smoothed the bottoms of my feet. Damp, hard, sand near the chilly ocean's edge, or soft, squishy, shifting warm sand had a give to it.

My feet were on the ground, whatever surface I was walking upon. Sometimes I strolled on the perfect-for-me surface. Other times, I was walking on a rougher, unforgiving surface. Choose your path and keep on walking.

You are a caregiver and learning priceless ways. Jot down what you've learned up to this point. You've learned much more than you think. Your lessons are things of beauty, because few are walking where you walk each day. Isn't it rich? Knowing what you know now.

Choose your favorite paths as much as possible. Be gentle. Be consistent. Keep going.

You've got this

Power time resonated with me. Others may call it daily quiet time, devotional time, or meditation time. Power time looks different person to person, but I'll share what mine included. I found it meaningful to read a Bible verse, think about it, meditate on it, and study it, then apply it to my life. If you don't plan, go through your day without your power time (even if it's a few minutes), you will be "doing" and your fulfillment at the end of the day will be minimal. How do I know this? I've watched people around me eliminate their power time.

And I've done it many times, as well.

My daily power time grows from my personal relationship with Jesus Christ. I talk. He talks, within my spirit. I listen. It's a tender, sweet, intimate time. I write three things I'm grateful for and three things I'm excited about, picturing each of those six items.

Journaling is also a habit you may want to try, if you're not already doing it. Journaling is a fancy word for writing or sketching your day, including your deep thoughts, questions, or emotions in a day. It could be a legacy to leave someone when your own life is said and done. You may think no one will want to read it. However, think of someone you love who has already passed. Wouldn't you love to read what they thought about at various times of their lives? Trust me. Someone will want to read your journals, and what a gift. You, finding your way in life.

Try planning your next day in the evening. You have more clarity, more than you will in the morning as you talk yourself out of what is your heart's desires, needs, or goals. After you plan the day, take a moment and assign the time each item will use. You will clearly see if you are over-planning your day. Allow time for yourself. Plan ahead. You've got this.

Let's talk a moment about self-confidence and the way it may play out in your life while caregiving. Are you wondering about your future or the future of your care recipient? Perfectly normal. However, the least anxiety is being present in this twenty-four-hour period. Slowing yourself to this twenty-four hours is easier if you focus on being in the present moment. When I had to do unpleasant tasks for Mom, I often thought of other wonderful images in my mind; before I knew it, the unpleasant task was done and Mom and I could move into our day. Your self-confidence will grow and before you know it, you will be a risk-taker and a hardy caregiver.

How does God speak to you? To your soul? He decided to make you in His own image. Imagine that. He loves you so much he gave His son to suffer excruciatingly in your place. None of us would give our sons. But God gave us His Son, Jesus, to free us, heal us, and give us life with Him forever. The One who sees. The One who guides. The One who loves you unendingly.

Were you thrown into caregiving? What if you were? At first, it's kind of glamorous, making all the decisions. It's all going like clockwork. You're extremely powerful and on top of things. Maybe you're the one who doesn't enjoy making quick decisions, but given the right amount of time to analyze, you make them. One month becomes three, six, nine, and now it's been a year, and you're more confident in caregiving.

Alone again

You may be the only one, as family and support people dropped off one by one. I called it the Flash in the Pan syndrome. They are there for the crisis and the new routines, but are wearied and depressed it's lasting so long. They no longer like the new paths of caregiving, and choose to not experience the emotional sadness, watching their loved one change. They eliminate regularly visiting the care recipient, thinking they have avoided the emotional pain of watching the care recipient in this "condition"--whatever dismal visions they picture in their head. These people are to be pitied the most, because at best, they are postponing the inevitable emotional pain. You, however, are a caregiver without regrets. They may have many regrets, guilt, shame; or start demanding money, furniture, or give you a piece of their minds, which often they cannot afford to do. You may hear all this as the care recipient is completing their final life purpose. Get out of God's way as He moves in other's lives. That's His job, not yours.

What are you the happiest about as a caregiver? What is your strength as a caregiver? Your brain will always search for answers, so ask yourself better questions than if you're caregiving the right or wrong way. This is your new life to experience and find your new ways.

Here & Now Reflection

SEVEN WORDS

Her voice was strong, happy, uplifting, encouraging, and able to tackle anything. I first remember my mom's voice when I was a "let me do it" busy three-year-old. Her voice was confident and certain. She was wanting to be fair with me. She was expecting obedience the first time she asked.

The next time I heard her voice, I was ten. She was wanting to help me. She did it the only way she knew, but hearing her voice that year was when I began shrinking in spirit; singled out, certain I was defective at my core. No amount of fixing could change it. I chose to internalize. I was damaged goods, less than, and too much all at the same time.

At thirteen-years-old, Mom's voice was quietly pleading with me for a closer relationship. But by then, I was like a stiff piece of leather. My heart wanted to chew small holes into the leather, so I was reachable, but I didn't know how. I often was doing the thing I didn't want to, acting the way I didn't want to, and speaking the way I didn't want to. Everything felt foreign to me. My mom's voice was constant. She was strong, resilient, and not one to be shoved to and fro.

At twenty-three-years-old, I heard her voice telling me in detail about her day while I was at work. At times I held the phone away from my ear, looking over at my best friend and saying "Uh-huh. Uh-huh." because it's all she required. She was in the telling mode. I don't recall her asking how my day was shaping up. I didn't realize it then, but the transition to caregiving was already taking place. When she was done, she might throw in "I love you" and happily went on with her day.

At forty-four-years-old, in the winter of her eighty-fifth year, her voice was music tickling my ears. Her tones were kind, appreciating, and relying on me. Unbelievably, I centered my days on hearing her voice, what she was thinking, needing, experiencing, and creating new ways to communicate with her.

At fifty-five-years-old, I heard her voice mostly in her eyes, without words. Love permeated everything between us during her ninety-sixth year. "She speaketh not; and yet there lies a conversation in her eyes"[1] was calligraphed above her headboard for me and visitors to remember.

Seven words describe my mom's essence:

Walking with God.

Loving.

Fun.

Fearless.

Servant.

---

1   https://quotes.yourdictionary.com/author/henry-wadsworth-longfellow/172903

Which quality intrigues you the most?

How could you apply it into your life this week?

MAKING CONNECTIONS

What's your love language? Communicating well as a caregiver with your care recipient is vital to vibrant, healthy relationships.

The Glitz

They stopped by and gave your care recipient a drink of water once in thirteen years. I saw them at a funeral.

"I gave your mom a drink of water. She was thirsty! You need to make sure she has water to drink. You really need to get on it!"

"Oh, thank you. Yeah, okay, uh-huh."

I dove into my deep forest green 1981 MGB sports car and sped away.

I did not have time for The Glitz. They slowed me down. I could give them mercy. They knew how lame and cheap their comments were, and it troubled them as they watched me caregiving day after day. No one saw. No one knew. No one wanted to know.

Be grateful for The Glitz. It was the most they could give. Stop judging. Caregiving scared them and they were unable to go the long haul with you.

Hug them. There will come a time when they will be a caregiver or care recipient, and learn not to be afraid. They were a spark with lots of feel-good phrasing, goofy advice, and warm fuzzies, but they left before the Short-Timer.

The Short-Timer

They promised they would be there for you day-after-day and check on your care recipient, if needed. And you counted on them for several years. However, long-term caregiving makes the Short-Timer too weary and too sad. And then one day, they were MIA. They didn't mean to, but they couldn't go the long haul. Perhaps another, non-caregiving task was better to ask of them; shopping, supplies, or a take-out meal. They were the Short-Timer. Give them grace. They had challenges of their own. Hug them. Love 'em anyway.

The Show-Off.

They bragged they greeted the care recipient. They watered a plant once. They boasted about talking with Mom's paid caregiver and they told them how well Mom was doing. Your care recipient was not doing well. Your days were long and dementia was a constant, now.

Always take the high road. Thank them for whatever they do. Be humble. Don't make it personal. It wasn't about you, anyway.

Resist

Resist the urge to become bitter about The Glitz, The Short-Timer, and The Show-Off. Above all, keep yourself at peace and keep loving others. Take no offense. Hold no grudges. Tell God about it. Ask forgiveness, if needed, and pour out grace, mercy, and most of all, genuine sincere love onto everyone in your path. Choose to be unable to resist.

Making connections

There are many ways to make connections, and here are a few I heard recently.

"I love your presence. You make me feel special and valued. I know you don't have lots of time, but when we're together for even a few minutes connecting, it is wonderful to me."

"Let's go to the beach. I love spending time with you. Thanks for giving me your whole day. It's such a blessing to my spirit."

"Let's hang out. I love the frivolous and the deep conversations we have."

Last Mother's Day, my adult children spent five hours visiting, eating, and playing card games with me. My love tank was overflowing.

My cousin, Linda, who lives in another state, uses the Marco Polo app. We send videos back and forth when it's convenient for each of us. Catching up with extended family is worth the effort.

Dating my future husband--one of the top three best decisions I ever made--we didn't want to be apart for long. Forty-seven years later, we still love each other's company. We silently work on projects, laugh, chat, or get together at the end of the day to catch up. We highly value connecting daily.

Use creativity with your care recipient. What is their love talk? They will tell you by their actions what love talk they use and whom they value most. Help them make their own connections.

Gifts of presence

On my forty-third birthday and upon retirement, Phil decorated around our hot tub with lovely palm trees.

"Surprise! We're going to Maui! You better start packing!" I joined him in the hot tub.

"What?! No way! Is Jordan, going?"

"Well, of course. We're all three going!"

"Yahoo! I can't believe you planned this and I didn't even have a hint!"

The great joy of presence. Recently, I invited Mom to ride along on coffee deliveries in Portland with me. She chose to stay in the car. She just wanted to be in my presence. Although my mom carried more of a servant's heart, she loved going places anytime, anywhere.

One day, I threw two large fold-up chairs, a round plastic basin, and a large plastic pitcher into my SUV, and helped Mom into the car. We arrived at Oceanside, where my parents owned a vacation home for much of my early childhood. We had a perfect view of waves crashing and rolling onto the shore. While she waited inside my car, I ran and scooped up sand, then helped her out of the car. I bundled her up with blankets, pivoted her to the chair, and gently sat her down. I removed her shoes and placed her feet in the warm sand.

"Ahhh…I can't believe you did this, Kay Nell. This is so cozy."

We sat side by side looking out at the sea, and it brought tears to my eyes.

I loved to surprise Phil and Jordan the most. I flew in Malcolm Smith and Tom Webb a couple of years. They are famous dirt bike motorcycle riders. They flew in to ride with Phil and his buddies and stay in our home. It was a gift of presence.

Touch and affirmations

Physical touch is a love talk language. I always bent down and gave Mom a kiss on her check when I arrived and left. At times, I'd sit beside her and hold her hand in silence. So simple. So impactful. So priceless.

With others I heard:

"Wow, I cannot believe all you can do and accomplish! You really rocked this. You should get an award." This was an affirmation I heard often at a company I worked.

"Which puppy do you want? This one or that one?" A generous gift from a best friend.

"For me?"

"Yes, I think you need a puppy, no strings attached."

Translate your care recipient's love talk into your caregiving day.

Remember when

One of Mom's best friends, Ida, wrote her after Mom was bedridden for several years.

"Remember when we went to Tennessee and we took a bus ride to see many fancy celebrity homes? We thought we would see the Johnny Cash Roundhouse. It was raining so hard and nearly dark. And the only thing we saw was a faint light in a couple of small windows and the bus driver almost went in the ditch.

Sailing to Hawaii for your eightieth birthday and you did the Charleston dance during the talent show. You were the hit of the evening! What a good time.

Do you remember you were going to learn to knit? Especially black Mohair yarn, which was fuzzy and impossible to rip; not much success there. Kay Nell did a better job. For many years we had some joyously fun times together. There was always something that we could do. We picked broccoli at Daisy's brother's farm and then we had to scald it and put it in the freezer. Never did that a second time.

Lots & lots of love & prayers, your friend, Ida."-- Mom and Ida are in heaven now.

Here & Now Reflection

HOPE

Three passengers embracing you as a caregiver are hope, faith, and courage. Faith sparks courage and gives you hope. Your care recipient is often experiencing a chaotic, confusing, physically painful and mentally exhausting time in their lives.

Maybe you didn't see caregiving coming and it hit you upside your head.

And you said, "What?!"

Your care recipient probably didn't see it coming either. Hope will keep you going when you don't think you can go any further and when the road ahead appears bleak. When it's hopeless, is when to welcome faith, vulnerability[2], and courage. If you are fearless (and you are), you will be full of hope. Not a silly-willy hope, but hope from the One who is the Author of Hope. Hope does not disappoint us. You are hopeful, full of faith, and exercising your courage muscles.

What are you the most hopeful about in your life today?

_____

_____

_____

2   https://www.netflix.com/title/81010166 Brené Brown

What is the last time you exercised faith?

_____

_____

When are you the most courageous?

_____

_____

FEELING ALIVE

One evening about 10:00pm, I came into Mom's apartment. She was wide-awake and alert. I transferred her into her manual wheelchair. We rode the elevator to the lobby and pushed her through the automatic sliding glass doors to the warm outside air. The summer evening sky was spectacularly lit up with stars and a full moon.

I pushed her close to a nearby bench and I sat with her in the warm air .We experienced God's painting in the sky. The stillness was full of His presence. Mom was gazing at the sky with the most peaceful, glowing smile on her face. We didn't speak. We held hands. After a long time, the window to her mind began dimming and I quietly, slowly, wheeled her back through the sliding doors, into the elevator, and transferred her gently back to bed. A sacred, late night memory with her. I still hold it inside my heart.

If Mom was asleep, I rarely woke her. I see it from a different view today. If I was sleeping, I'd want Jordan or Nicole to wake me up. I could sleep anytime, and Mom could, too. She loved my presence. I offered grace to myself, as I did my best with what I knew at the time. I was making detailed maps while I traveled on this unknown caregiving path to share with others.

Time is short

No one knows how much time we have in our lives. You cannot recapture it once time is spent. One thing is certain, we are breathing today. This minute. This second. How are you spending your time? Are you like me, and sometimes make plans far into the future? Then your mind is cluttered and you can barely sleep? You've missed the daily journey. Many changes and growth spurts may be needed as you add caregiving into the mix of your life. God renews. God replenishes. God restores. You're right on time with Him. Use your time connecting with words or quiet moments with those you love.

Vacations always moved at sloth speed for me. I went two hundred miles per hour most of the time at work. Vacation came--unstructured, vast quantities of time. A couple days of unwinding, and I found my groove. Time always zipped by for me at work.

How about you? When does time go slow for you? When does it zip by? How many appointments do you schedule during a day? Are your responsibilities tearing you away from caregiving? Is duty pushing you into caregiving? Some days I relaxed, slowed down, and soaked my mom's feet; gave her a pedicure; slathered lotion on her. She never would have scheduled a pedicure before her stroke. She thought it frivolous, a waste of time. This apple fell far from that tree, as I bask in a good pedicure, manicure and massage; more of a necessity than a luxury for me. My best friend, Bobi, taught me the joys of all three in my third decade. She was right, and I've never changed my mind. My weekly massage is a gift I enjoy giving myself.

"Let's play some racquetball!"

My friend and I often did. Exercise relieved my stressors, and I became a better caregiver.

Other friends gave their unasked for advice.

"Let's go out to lunch!"

"No, I can't. I need to go check on Mom."

"I thought you just left there."

"Yes, but I need to make sure she's okay, so I don't have time to go to lunch."

This, my friend, created undue stress on me. I didn't make much time for renewal.

If you continue to give, give, give--without replenishing yourself--excess stress, depression, and burnout will become close enemies. You cannot take care of everyone. Allow yourself time to rest, renew and recuperate. How much time do you need to re-energize yourself? What do you enjoy when you are not in the role of a caregiver? Caregiving can take all the hours of your day, if you allow it. Perhaps you choose a day or more for yourself. No one is coming to rescue you and tell you to take time off. Only you can give yourself permission.

Enjoy and make the most of the time taking care of yourself. Maybe it's one day a month, one day a week or a daily hour to rejuvenate. Away from phones, television, movies, and all the ways you distract from good company with yourself. Schedule it. If spa salons are your thing, do it! There needs to be a time you renew spiritually, physically, emotionally and mentally. A little meditating time, a nature walk, giving grace and mercy to yourself as gifts. Create beautiful mental images and imagine they are happening. Your thoughts, words, and actions create your future. Welcome faith into your life.

> *"Now faith is the reality of what is hoped for,*
> *the proof of what is not seen."*
> HEBREWS 11:1 (CSB)

Start a new project making you feel alive and creative. Replenish yourself. Experiment with who you are, apart from your caregiving role. God is multi-dimensional. It's how He made you. He made you for creativity. Come up alongside your Creator and see what He's creating in you.

Time for memories

Bring your talents to make memories with your loved one.

Maybe it's reading a book out loud. I helped my best friend's mom by reading a book she'd started and wanted to finish while she was in the hospital doing the business of dying.

She'd say, "Read slower."

I did. We finished it. She thoroughly enjoyed the story only she knew. A short time later she went to her heavenly home.

I quickly gave voice to the vision I saw clearly in my mind.

"Go! I can see Him. He's waiting for you. Do you see Him? His hands are outstretched in love to welcome you home."

She took a deep breath and went to Him.

Your caregiving time is priceless, sweet and rich. Time you are giving out to your care recipient, who cannot do for themselves in some way.

Mom had memorized many Bible verses and songs after she gave her life to Jesus Christ when she was eighteen years of age, a soon-to-be new bride.

She was in her ninth decade now. One of the last scriptures she knew by heart, and we recited together, was Psalm 23—"The Lord is my shepherd; I shall not want. He makes me to lie down in green pastures. He leads me beside the still waters. He restores my soul...." Psalm 23:1-3a (NKJV)

Movers brought my upright 1900 Sears piano to her room, about three feet from the end of her bed. She'd paid for my piano lessons for twelve years and loved to hear me play. She loved hearing my brother, Jim, play the most and I did, too. His boogie-woogie was always a hit with audiences. My specialty was Christian and classical music. Mom and I sang while I played her favorite songs "My God and I"--"In the Garden"--"What a Friend We Have in Jesus"--and "How Great Thou Art"--which I can barely sing sometimes even yet, many years after she's gone to be with the Lord. I loved her deeply, enjoyed priceless moments, and the caregiving with her was worth every tough day.

Free your mind

Last Thursday, Laps of Love's, Dr. Lori, came to my home to euthanize my beloved Old English Sheepdog, Norm, who was suffering prematurely from a terminal disease. Our family went to the burial site for a memorial. A few hours later, my housekeepers came to work their magic, while I drove to my masseuse for some relaxation. A bright spot amidst the turmoil of losing Norm. A writing class followed for two hours in my office. By the evening, my mind was not freed; it was tangled like a spider's web. Too much was scheduled in my day while experiencing such grief, too.

Decide what your limits are for your personal schedule. You may want to do it all. Something may burst open and it might be you. Choose well and be selective. Wherever you are, be completely present; in the moment. Speak life to those around you. Free them and yourself.

Make a list. You may fight making lists. Do it anyway. Place your tasks and appointments in a calendar. Random living is great, but does not work well as a caregiver, visiting a care recipient here and there. Writing it down frees your mind.

I made a list of the seven tasks I needed to accomplish before doing anything else. Every morning, other fun things called my name. I continued doing the seven tasks. This gave me peace of mind entering my day, and a better attitude, too. My list of seven freed my mind and kept me on track.

Caregiving is not always working in your strengths. Some tasks will definitely be a weakness and weakness is where character growth happens. Humbly ask for help. Delegating to family, friends, or other caregivers on your team may be helpful. Be relentlessly brave if you are the primary caregiver for your parents. It will take all your courage digging into your toolbox of resources. Keep your toolbox open. Use new tools, not always reaching for the same ones. Free your mind.

There are days you will be exhausted and feel alone. You are not alone. Your close friends see you. God never leaves you and never forsakes you. He sees you. He knows you. He loves you. You can invite others to jump in and help, in a myriad of ways. When someone jumps in, celebrate! You freed them to work in their strength and freed your own mind and body.

Splitting time

When I started as a caregiver, I never dreamed it would be over a decade. Emotional, yes. I wished I'd spent less time worrying, less time obsessing, and less time with anxiety over Mom's daily care. I learned from my mistakes.

Walk a slower gait and you will avoid burn out. Think about the amount of time you have as a caregiver. Take into account your family, your children, your friends, and yourself. Emergencies will arise, but you can handle them. You are doing great. I'm so proud of you. Courageous, you are (I say in my best Yoda voice).

If you are consumed by caregiving, a project, or a challenge, do them wholeheartedly, with a joyful heart. We all have twenty-four hours. Get enough sleep. In my thirties, I slept five or six hours a night and drove to our coffee-roasting business at four in the morning. I loved it. Now, thirty-five years later, last night I slept nine hours. My attitude and my energy were at a premium. Nine hours doesn't happen every night, but I know the amount of sleep I need.

Caregiving can overtake your life, if you let it. It can consume your life, keeping all the balls in the air, but eventually they crash down because your caregiving was never meant to consume your life. You have many demands and things you love to do.

I love spending time with Jordan, his wife, Nicole, and my husband, Phil. They are the most important people in my world. Early years, I was confused how to split my time caregiving and still make our young family the number one priority. I didn't want to miss any special moments with them. Caregiving often interrupted the fun things I was enjoying.

Jordan often came with me to his grandma's assisted-living facility. I often felt guilty for him experiencing time there, as it was emotionally sad for me. However, I left guilt behind and created new ideas for Jordan's visits and he learned to adapt. Since my mom's bed was in the living room next to my piano, Jordan often wandered into the bedroom where Mom's hoyer lived. He sat in Mom's hoyer netting and pumped the hoyer handle to elevate himself high in the air. I laughed when I saw what he could do. He played in an extra wheelchair and learned wheelies. If your kids need to spend extra time with your care recipient, let them play in the midst of the heaviness of caregiving.

Three of Mom's nine siblings came by to visit with coffee and cake at an outside table. Jordan sat about five feet away and softly played his guitar as background music. If some of your family must go with you, as you are a caregiver, think outside the box and create fun environments for the young and the elderly.

God was definitely calling me to be a caregiver for my mom. I hoped he was calling someone…anyone else. Through many tears I knew He took past failures and made them into successes. I trusted He was doing that again. I was on the right path. So are you. You are not late. You are right on time.

Turning away

I ran away from watching intense suffering and my own emotional pain in my twenty-ninth year, when Mom's second husband was dying. Oh, no one knew it. I coordinated meals to be brought in for Mom and visitors. I was supportive. When it came down to the last twenty-four hours though, I ran.

I'm not proud of it, still to this day. I knew he was going to die that night. I ran anyway. I chose not to face the intense suffering and my own emotional pain, drove back home, and uncharacteristically, drank myself to sleep. Phil stayed with Mom and her dying husband the entire night. Her husband passed near daybreak.

Many years had passed when I chose to be Mom's caregiver. I knew it in my core. This time, I wasn't running, no matter where the path led. I helped her through pain, mental confusion and made tough decisions when she could not. Excessive drinking was no longer an option. I trusted the only One who gave me strength for each day. He became my 'why'.

Your why

What's your why? What is God calling you to in your life? I'm pretty sure it's not mall browsing, grocery shopping, social media, or another Netflix/Amazon binge. Don't wince if he's asking you to do a hard thing, one you're not comfortable doing. Character growth happens there.

He equips you for every good work. He didn't give it to me ahead of time, but prepared and equipped me little by little. I never grew when I was comfortable, only when I was out of my comfort zone. As I wrote that last sentence, I realized once again, He's calling *me* out of a recent comfort zone. You're not alone.

Mom looked at me one day and decided to talk.

"You look great in your outfit, Kay Nell. You're so pretty."

I looked behind me. She must be talking to someone else. No one there. Only me.

"Thanks, Mom!"

How beautiful it was God helped us finish well, moment by moment, day by day, through the thirteen years.

Jordan was an intern/sleeper at a firehall for several years, attending on numerous fire and medical calls. The time he watched me as a caregiver helped shape his attitudes on future medical calls and his ability to help people more effortlessly. God always surprises me.

I didn't see the benefits that came for Jordan. I thought I was wrecking him. God was forming his heart for future opportunities. I never imagined the benefits of Jordan watching me as a caregiver when it was the hardest thing I ever did. Jordan benefitted, and in hindsight, I saw a larger view of the 'why' in caregiving for Mom.

Grab your favorite drink. Find a couple pieces of paper and a pen. Get comfy. Discover your own 'why'.

Why did you decide to be a caregiver?

Why did you decide not to be a caregiver?

What are you unwilling to give up as a caregiver?

What does God's truth have to say about it?

What about caregiving scares you the most?

What about caregiving draws you to do it, even if it's not your strength?

This may be the most important work you'll do today. Unconditional love was my reason to be a caregiver. It was my personal response for the decades of unconditional love, godly teaching, and serving she sowed deeply into my life. We were finishing up our lives together. I was determined to have no regrets and to finish well with her. I was not a natural caregiver. Instead, I used my strengths first. When my strengths no longer served me as a caregiver, I trusted God, and my character grew by leaps and bounds as I gave care outside my comfort zone. It wasn't pretty. It wasn't easy. But it was worth everything.

What details concern you, concern your Father God. I love Him, don't you? He calls us to finish well. He will be there every step of the way. Will it be easy? Probably not. All sorts of emotions are wrapped into caregiving. I dug deep. I'm confident you will, too.

Mom progressed and rarely spoke. I looked into her eyes and knew the conversation at any given moment. I knew her dark brown eyes, her body language, and her loving lectures by heart. I knew her core values and what she did not value. She talked to me over and over again with her expressive eyes and years together.

God cares about every detail of our lives. He wants us to communicate and establish an intimate relationship with Him. I am fully known by Him. When I hear Him in my spirit I want to answer a resounding, "YES!"

Are you discovering your 'why' or missing it for the distractions calling your name today? Give yourself grace to eliminate or add the things you value deeply. They are part of your 'why'; your focus is less likely to change, and you will be living your life with greater purpose.

Five senses

When you are in the caregiving mode, be a caregiver. Give it your all. When you are away, there's no need to think about it anymore. It may be a challenge. Move your body. Get outside. Go for a walk. Look around you. Daily miracles are right in front of you. Pull some weeds. Plant a flower. Pick some flowers. Watch the birds. Listen to the sounds around you.

Try this fun, simple practice on a walk:

Five things you can see around you.

Touch four things you can see around you.

Three things you hear.

Two things you can smell.

One thing you can taste.

You did it! You slowed yourself down, diminished anxiety, and basked in your life. I'm not a natural nature-lover, but it is fun practicing gardening, watching birds, picking raspberries.

I live in a large forest with gray squirrels, chipmunks, coyotes, bobcats, bats, blue jays, hawks, vultures, geese, hummingbirds, yellow chickadees, and a loving ninety-three-pound Old English Sheepdog with the registered name, "Norm of Courageous Spirit." If you saw him, he was less than a courageous spirit. I'm not always courageous, either. Sometimes it takes a while to live up to our given name. "Rejoicer/Pure Light" is what my name means. I did not earn the name. The only way I can receive the name is through the redeeming work of the Cross of Jesus Christ.

Teaching by doing

Each Christmas, mom drove my brother, Jim, and I to visit the elderly from our church; ones who now spent their days in their homes or in nursing homes. This was way before assisted-living facilities. Many didn't receive visitors and most were put on a shelf by their families.

Let me begin where we did, making miniature breads and baking them in metal orange juice cans. We slid them out, rolled them up in foil and red curling ribbon around each rotund bread. The three of us anticipated the baking and our journey to fifty elderly, housebound people, whom Mom chose. Most were kid-friendly; talking with us, showing us fun things and digging out small candies for my brother and me. We were richer from giving to others, who had so many needs and increasingly lonely—the kind of lonely even a small child felt when it was time to say goodbye.

Mom taught us by doing. She didn't talk about baking breads, didn't talk about the delivery week, and didn't talk about the time it all took. She taught us by doing, and she had a strong heart for the elderly.

Life is happening

Jordan named our calico cat Blue, because he felt-tip painted his kitty paw blue. He wanted no one to take his favorite kitten as they perused our kitten litter. Blue shamelessly delivers daily gifts to our back door with long meowing bragging rights. Look around you and see life happening. Beautiful life.

Caregiving is often all-consuming, but you are the most important person needing self-care. No one is going to give you permission to do it. If walking is painful some days, lift weights, do one hundred sit-ups, take a Zoom class, increase your heart rate, swim, play music, or garden.

I finally planted carrots, and they seem to be full grown at one-half inch long and one-eighteenth inch wide. Lettuce, thyme, and sage were my success stories, and I cut them several times this summer. I am more of an entrepreneurial spirit. Whatever you choose, select ways to rejuvenate yourself. Guilt is from the enemy. Conviction is from the Holy Spirit living in you, and always brings love and hope fast behind. God made you and said how very, very good you are. If it lines up with His Word, you go for it. I'm so proud of you. You are relentlessly virtuous. Life is happening all around you. Reach out and watch for it.

Here & Now Reflection

I SEE YOU

I see you. You are not alone. You are now in the club. A club no one wants to be in. Or maybe you couldn't wait to join the club, and caregiving is your passion. Either way I see you. You are not alone. I know what you've been doing. You've been caregiving on the lovely days and the challenging days. You get surprised frequently. I'm so proud of your great courage and how you are growing and stretching yourself.

Even after others leave, you're there, doing what you do so the care recipient's life is the best it can possibly be. I see you. I don't care if you view it as your duty to God and Country. I see you.

Caregiving for my mom was thirteen years, twenty-two days. I was surprised frequently and so was she. On God's radar, I was seen. And I see you, too. You have grit.

Is there anything you are running away from currently?

What did you discover about why you are a caregiver?

_____

_____

What relationships are you willing to see to the end?

_____

_____

RUNNING HARD

"Take care of yourself! Go see your mom a couple times a month, not every day!"

I didn't have time for a friend's nonsensical advice. I needed tools, resources and stamina. I began finding my way. I winged it, as many of you have up to this point. All the tools you need are in your hands. Many emergency situations came up day after day in caregiving for Mom.

Wolves can run for miles and miles at seven to eight miles per hour, and up to thirty miles per day, without tiring. They have stamina. Cheetahs can run fifty to eighty miles per hour for about three miles. They stop to rest to prevent overheating. Their endurance is limited.

I usually ran with the wolves during my mom's changing health and emergencies. Caregiving for Mom drove me to excellence and long hours. When possible, I paced myself more like a cheetah with short spurts of endurance, with time to rest and recuperate. It won't be easy, but you will know deep down your care giving is shaping you, and you will find yourself welcoming it.

Don't misunderstand me. I played racquetball several times a week, met close friends for coffee, and took a few vacations. Even doing self-care, you will often feel like you're running with the wolves. But then, wolves are persevering and resilient, too.

Oh, but a lion runs short distances at fifty miles per hour, leaps as far as thirty-six feet and are social animals.

> … *"lion, king of animals,*
> *who won't turn aside for anything"*…
> PROVERBS 30:30 (NLT)

I prefer to be a lion. Unwavering in my walk with God.

Simplest choices

I've made a lot of good choices, agonizing choices, and poor choices in my life. Come before God with your choices. He will meet you there. He cares about every detail of your life. This morning, Phil and I drove to the beach and picked up five cases of freshly canned albacore tuna on the fishing docks and to share with friends.

Lord, I need someone to put the five heavy cases in my car for me. Provide someone there.

"Kay Nell Miller for five cases of tuna."

"Oh, yes. Wait a moment. I need to wash my hands first. I'll get them right away." Out she came with the five cases. It's hard for me to ask for help.

"Is there anyone who could put the cases in my car, perhaps?"

"Oh, sure! We'd be glad to."

Two young women jerked up the cases like tooth-picks and slid them into my trunk.

"Thank you so much. You made my day!"

"You're welcome. We're glad to do it!"

I took money from my purse.

"Carrying those tuna cases meant so much to me today. Thank you."

They looked shocked.

"Thank you!"

God provided two strong women to put the cases into my car. I'd always carried them out myself and could feel the results of it for hours. What a caring, detailed Lord.

Choices. Are you remembering some of yours, now? The great ones. The agonizing ones. The poor ones. What choices are you considering in your own life? Job change? Relationship change? Spiritual change? Thought life change? Nutrition change? What to clean first? What project to start? All change creates tension in some degree.

Whatever changes you are considering, it doesn't matter if you don't have all the answers yet. You will. Do the next thing in front of you and you're on your way. Again, you do not need all the answers to your unknowns before you take the first step. You are smart. You will figure it out on the way. People will come into your life once you start down the caregiving path. Choose wisely. It will fall into place as you start your journey. Adventures await. Oh yes--and great courage. He never leaves you. Ever.

Whatever you like

I've made selfish choices. Not even considering others in my life. Bent on getting my own way. My poorest choices always sing the same song: I want what I want when I want it. Reminds me of a song[3] "You Can Have Whatever You Like" by T.I.

One season in my life, God and I were having an intimate conversation on the couch in my mom's duplex, before her cold days of dementia. I heard Him in my spirit clearly. I boldly told him about a thing I wanted to do. It was one of my most selfish talks with Him. I wished it had been the only selfish conversation with Him. But He knew me. He wasn't surprised by my boldness. I asked what He thought.

He was clear in my spirit.

"No."

It was a quiet no, but a solid one.

"Yeah, well I think I'm doing it anyway. It doesn't matter, really. I'll be fine. I know it's a good decision for me right now.

Pride had raised its ugly head, making me extremely aggressive and doing what I thought best. When I hear someone say something similar within my earshot now, I cringe. The price I paid for boldly going my own way was high, but He gently guided me, taught me, and reminded me how much He loved me. As long as I said, "Yes, Lord" I knew good was coming, regardless of what it looked like to anyone else. Today if I brought up that memory with God,

---

3   https://www.youtube.com/watch?v=Kgdr2uytpDI

He'd say, "I don't know what you're talking about." I have a clean slate and you can, too.

"No discipline seems enjoyable at the time, but painful. Later on, however, it yields the fruit of peace and righteousness to those who have been trained by it."
HEBREWS 12:11 (CSB)

"I pondered the direction of my life, and I turned...".
PSALM 119:59 (NLT)

Hard places

I remember the day I asked Him.

"What are you teaching me in this hard place?"

I was caregiving for Mom, and each day when I left her place, I often stood in the hallway, tears rolling down my cheeks. She had windows of lucidity, followed by speaking with her eyes only to me. We knew each other well.

Years later, God's quiet, gentle voice spoke to my spirit again.

"I'm teaching you not to run when things get hard. You're staying this time."

I wept as He gave me opportunities to trust Him and change old patterns. He broke me so gently, I hardly knew it was happening. Oh, there was emotional pain: many days and nights of tears and exhaustion, watching Mom's mind slowly slip away, but He was always there with me. I sensed His presence the most in her room.

It must have broken his heart to hear me tell him I

thought I knew what was best, and not accept the wisdom of God Almighty, King of Kings, all those years ago. He didn't yell. He didn't leave me. He didn't throw a fit. He didn't even turn His head away. He lovingly waited.

He did many miracles in my life in the days ahead. He was teaching me not to run away when things were difficult. He knew my future. I saw a minute. He saw my lifetime. He forgave me way back then, before I even told Him how sorry I was, or wanted to change direction. He knew this lesson was a critical one for my future and in my spiritual walk with Him. I'm so grateful and humbled that God took the time to kindly teach me. Over time, I became happily surrendered to Him and peace came.

Bigger than dementia

I strolled from my green Honda sedan (sold the sports car to get Mom in a car) through the automatic glass double doors, into the lobby on my way to the cafeteria for the umpteenth time for Mom's lunch. She could no longer feed herself, and I often fed her when she was confined to bed.

Before I reached the cafeteria door, a frail, silver-haired lady in her manual wheelchair put her hand out to me. I stopped in my tracks and reached my hand out to greet her, as we exchanged smiles. She held my hand and looked intently into my blue-gray eyes.

"Girl, you know God loves you so very much. You are on the right track. Keep going. He's with you."

Her Aussie accent made me smile. Later, I asked a caregiver about her.

"Her name is Vivian. Her mind is never lucid."

Oh, but God had other things in mind for Vivian and I. She was one hundred percent had a lucid mind with me. She prophesied to me on a normal day, on my way to the cafeteria. How many more has she ministered to from her wheelchair?

Never discount a frail, silver-haired lady, stuck in her wheelchair during the winter of her life, able to speak prophetic words over you. Be daring. God has exciting, divine appointments for you in the midst of routine days. It's right there in front of you.

Top best choices

Okay. The top best three choices I made from my first decade to my sixth decade of living were:

At the age of six I accepted Jesus as my Savior and my best friend. I never changed from the choice made at such a young age. I knew He was mine and no one could take Him from me.

At nineteen years of age, I married the love of my life within two years. We're celebrating nearly fifty years together.

At the age of thirty-seven, after eighteen years of marriage, Jordan was born.

These three choices shaped my life, blessed my life, and moved me forward. God never left me, even when I could not feel him or see him. He was there with His face toward me as he was loving and welcoming me. I didn't earn His love. He freely gave it. I'm not special. He freely gives it to all who accept Him.

As you are a caregiver, He sees you when no one else knows or understands what you are going through. Are you seeking His face? Are you watching for ways you see Him at work? He's there with you, and good things are in store for you. As you embrace Him, you are heroic; your great adventure is only beginning. Watch for your own daily mini-miracles. They are often found in the most obscure places.

"He (Jesus) replied, What is impossible with men is possible with God."
LUKE 18:27 (CSB)

Here & Now Reflection

ADVOCACY

Advocacy is power and always creates flow. You are doing what you know your care recipient's wishes are while they are in your care. You are their voice. What a privilege it is to exercise it. Do not hesitate to speak up. Even though you may often need to stand your ground in advocating, creating flow between the care recipient, caregiver, and the third person you may be meeting with is always the goal. Advocacy is support for, arguing for, calling for, pushing for, pressing for, and defending a person unable to do so for themselves. Advocacy is ensuring people who are the most vulnerable in society have their voices heard and their rights defended.

What ways are you an advocate for your care recipient currently?

How could you improve your advocacy for your care recipient?

List the tiny miracles you saw today.

_____

_____

What are your top three best life choices up until now?

_____

_____

RUNNING THICK

Mom was searching for the perfect pair of shoes (not hurting the bunions on her feet). I took time off work to take her to the appointment; she used a walker at the time. Everywhere we went took twice as long, and this day was no exception. I parked, went to the trunk, lifted her rolling walker out, and brought it to the passenger side of the car. She lifted her feet out of the car, rotated to the right and slowly stood upright for a minute, then snail-paced it to the store door, with me walking alongside her. I propped open the store's heavy door while standing by in case Mom lost her balance.

She tried on a few shoes with a kind gentleman helping, but she couldn't focus on selecting one. She had a tough time making choices, so I tried to help her select one by asking simple questions.

"Mom, does this pair fit you well?"

"I wish you'd shut up! Why don't you go to the car and let me handle this!"

The kind gentleman looked like he wanted to melt into the floor. I was melting, too. My patience was running thin, and my frustration was running thick.

I slowly walked out the door with my composure intact, sauntered to my car, opened my car door, and stopped. It hit me like a brick, realizing she was mentally unable to write checks, open the store's door to leave, or maneuver the steps alone. Reluctantly, I returned and sat by her in the store, calmly waiting for her to select the most comfortable shoe. I was embarrassed she yelled at me and confused at her levels of anger. I took it personally. I felt badly for asking her questions and felt defective again, inside (an old habit of mine from childhood).

This shoe day was in the very earliest stage of dementia; I didn't understand, and it was tough to accept her subtle personality change. When I helped her back into the car, it was as if nothing happened in the store. She was back to her kind, grateful self. She found a good pair of shoes that fit, and I experienced more moments that didn't fit.

Basic teamwork

Transporting a care recipient takes teamwork. An ambulatory care receiver is easier to transport to appointments and visits to relatives or friends. If incontinent, place a waterproof mattress pad under them in the seat of your vehicle or wheelchair. If they are not completely ambulatory, a push travel wheelchair, powerchair, rolling walker or riding scooter may be required. If in an assisted-living facility, there is an accessible bus available to take residents to medical appointments, shopping, salons, etc. If the care recipient is in bed most of the time, the nurse at the facility could call the doctor, explain the condition, and no one needs to go anywhere (which may be preferable at some point). If the nurse doesn't want to make the call, speak to the doctor's nurse directly for help.

If you're transporting, check if the equipment fits into your vehicle and if not, call for local medical transport. When Mom could not walk, I transferred her from a manual push wheelchair to my car and crammed it into the trunk. I became a ninja master at transferring. I tried using a hoyer to place her in my car once, rather than using my back. It didn't work, as it did not clear the hood of the car. The hoyer does work if the vehicle is a convertible. And how much fun would it be for the care recipient and you!

It's important to keep appointments. If medical transport in some form is used, the caregiver is free to ride along, or drive your own car and meet the transport at the location. If the care recipient manages appointments on their own, enjoy a little bit of respite. If using a bus at an assisted-living facility, the wait for pick-up may be long and hard on your care recipient. A personal, local medical transport usually costs $50 or more, but I found their promptness was well worth the cost. Waiting for the facility bus or any transport to return for the care recipient after an appointment is a must for the caregiver. Try to schedule appointments on the same day so it does not become cumbersome for your care recipient to go out multiple days.

If they are able, allow the care recipient to talk at the appointment and tell their story to the doctor. It will help to give the doctor a written description of any challenges the care recipient has experienced. The care recipient's view, due to dementia, may be completely different than what is reality. It's kind to write the description, rather than dispute what the care recipient has said or not said to the doctor.

Reality now

Often a care recipient with dementia has a version of what is going on, and the caregiver has a reality view. They may become belligerent and angry with you. This will rarely be a one-time event. Put on your thick skin. They may even choose a group setting, and you may become embarrassed. It is not about you; this is their reality now. You must adapt. Try to be gracious. A soft answer can de-escalate. If needed, get into their world and agree with them.

You may be the responsible one. The one who takes them to all the appointments. The one procuring the medicine. Perhaps you even volunteered to be the responsible one. Exercise patience. Traveling to an appointment is an outing for them. Your care recipient may move slowly or find distracting details.

"Look! A bird! It's so pretty. Watch it."

For many, this is their only freedom trip for the entire month. Allow yourself plenty of time. Excessive time. Help them enjoy their outing, even if, in reality, it is the most boring or stressful doctor appointment ever for you.

"Let's go out to eat. I'll pay. Let's go!"

You may not be hungry. Go anyway. This is part

of their outing and they want to make it a pleasant journey. Live in the moment, then go home to relax, renew, and rejuvenate.

Here & Now Reflection

CONTINUITY

Keep the continuity of your life on an even keel, and do not allow caregiving to overtake your life completely. It may be challenging, but it is worth the effort. Please don't isolate your children from the care recipient, or your caregiving. Children watch what you do more than what you say. Caregiving is teaching them compassion, serving, decision-making, and love.

If you're working outside or inside the home, your time is limited and valuable. Keep some evenings for yourself, even if you need to hire other caregivers. Your life needs shape and definition, along with joy, laughter, and creativity.

If you're retired and caregiving, carve time out to recharge your batteries; leave the caregiving behind for a few days. No matter how you look at it, time is short for you and for your care recipient. Make the most of your days.

Find a creative activity that makes you lose track of time. And no, I don't mean talking on your phone, typing on your computer, or swiping your phone through the latest social media news. As we age, we can lose zest and purpose. We need a reason to arise full of vitality in the morning, anticipating what opportunity lies waiting for us. Experiment and find your niche.

What makes you lose track of time?

What's your purpose for getting out of bed in the morning?

How would you have made better choices than I did during the shoe story?

PAYING
ATTENTION

I need to catch up on a 365- day devotional. I'm behind on Day 3. I got a new washer and dryer. I can hardly wait to read the manual and do a load of laundry. I sure hope they work; they're much more high tech than any I've had. So grateful we could go get them. It's raining, and my computer cords are outside. Glad I put a plastic bag on to protect them.

Here comes my Old English Sheepdog. My office chair was raised but it's incredibly high. My feet don't touch solid ground. Norm wants to be petted and keeps nudging my arm.

I have shorts on and am getting cold on my legs outside. I need a drink of water, but I'm on Zoom and don't want to distract others. This tea is getting cold. I love my new pen. Hoping it doesn't give out while I'm writing. It has an imitation crystal piece at the top.

I do love bling. I like the way it flows across paper smoothly, yet controllably. Where is my other pen? I know I brought it outside with me. Where is it? Gophers are really busy with the ground so soft right now. Norm won't catch them, but his dog buddy, Otto, will. I wonder if…

Racing thoughts

Gray squirrels are beautiful and rampant in our forest. They dart, chatter, and bury nuts in the dirt for winter. Our squirrels became distracting when some of the tops of our mature fir trees became like sticks in the air. What was more distracting was the county extension office telling us the gray squirrel sometimes do that when they are expecting baby squirrels or just because they want to eat the tree tops.

Distracting thoughts. You have your own stories. My thoughts raced within a few seconds to a myriad of distractions avoiding the things God desired me to do. I knew writing was what I needed to be doing this morning. I found many side tracked distractions instead.

Your thing may not be pens, dogs, squirrels, or gophers, but the enemy of our soul still distracts you in ways that stop the joy-filled life from bubbling up in you. A friend of mine primps before a mirror for twenty minutes in the middle of the day—slowly brushing her hair into place, adding mascara, lipstick, a spritz of cologne, gazing at her reflection, and starting the process again if she deemed necessary. Twenty minutes later, she emerged from the mirror. I was done in one minute and accomplished all my primping. Racing thoughts are personalized for each individual. I don't enjoy primping, so I make it quick and easy. It doesn't mean I'm right or wrong, it's just preferences.

The Accuser used well-worn paths of distractions, worry, and fear to keep me from my God-ordained, life-giving paths. My God is greater, but speaking His truth aloud, and giving my heart to Him moment by moment is the path to shut the Accuser up. He shrinks and flees at the name of Jesus. My life did not go perfectly as a caregiver, but He did give me strength and grace.

What are your distractions? There was a 1,000-piece bird puzzle on the table today, and we were distracted to find the next piece and lock it into place. Time stood still. Before I knew it, I was running late.

TV was another one of my distractions. There was a great show on TV. Who am I kidding? It could be a lousy show, and I numbly sat and zoned out. I'm late for an event, rushing to accomplish because I was distracted with the unimportant. Do I really need to research everything about an actor?

Distractions can be useful, however. In the dentist's chair with air buds, listening to music or a podcast was a fantastic way to distract myself. Our minds think at an extremely rapid rate. Parts of our brain take half a second for sensory input from outside to become a conscious experience.[4]

As Mom's caregiver, I've changed a myriad of unexpected incontinent diapers, catheterized her, cleaned up bowel movements, processed laundry, brushed food-stuck teeth, placed bibs, fed her meals, gave nebulizer treatments, flushed ear wax, bandaged bedsores, showered her, administered pedicures, manicures, massages (when I had no idea what I was doing), replaced oxygen cannulas, cleaned concentrator filters, and cradled her in my arms.

---

4 https://nymag.com/speed/2016/12/what-is-the-speed-of-thought.html

In a good way, I used distracting thoughts: engaged my imagination by singing a song or talking about fun moments with Mom to alleviate the intensity of the caregiving tasks at hand. Distracting was a handy resource. Wisdom is knowing when a distraction is useful or when it is procrastination.

Pay attention

I might have missed it. Mom was smiling, softly speaking life-giving words to me on her way through dementia. When the caregivers in a facility were not keeping her clean, I was paying attention. When another one carved a knife drawing into the mahogany wood of my piano, I was paying attention. Please pay attention every day.

Two elderly gals, in a diminished physical and mental state, found each other in front of a toasty fireplace. Warm cloth gloves worn while holding hands, napping, chatting, and laughing. Their joy splashes onto me as I walk by. They are there every afternoon in the assisted-living facility. Two best girlfriends who are right on time with Him. He opened my eyes to see their joy and connection on a mundane day going to visit Mom. Pay attention.

Caregiving is demanding, but a deeply worthwhile position. You do it in obscurity, often. No one is watching you. No one understands except another caregiver. My path crossed many paid caregivers, but never a caregiver for family. You are seen by God. Every tear. Every joy. Every mundane task. He is paying attention.

Phil and I were caregivers for our parents and their spouses. Family caregivers were out there, but they were not in our view. In my view were families sporadically visiting their loved ones, but not caregiving. Stick with it. Perhaps one day you will be a care recipient, and you may need your own caregiver for a short time.

What time of day do you distract yourself the most? What are you trying to avoid? Jot down your thoughts about your distractions. Do you need to set the distraction aside for now or embrace it? I'm so proud of all the hard work you are doing as a caregiver. You are paying attention.

Here & Now Reflection

SUFFICIENT FOR TODAY

You are enough. You are sufficient for today. No need to toughen up. You understand enough. You have enough time. You know how to solve any challenge you face today. You already have the answers you're searching for. Tap into your resources.

If you wait until you can do things perfectly, procrastination takes over. You're practicing. When you know more, you will be practicing new skills. You don't need to arrive at some perfection level. Practice.

What you accomplish and what you say is enough. You are not too much. You are perfect the way you are today. You persevere and exercise great courage.
What challenge are you needing answers about? Brainstorm resources available.

You may have laughed at my distractions. What distractions resonate with you?

Are you uncomfortable before or after a decision is made?

What new skill are you willing to practice?

PADDLING ALONG

My cell phone rang. *Another sales call, I bet!*

"Is this Kay Nell Miller?"

"Yes. Who's this?"

"This is the chaplain at St. Charles Hospital in Bend. Your husband is here."

"Is he okay?"

"Well, they're working on him."

"Is he okay? Let me talk to his nurse."

"She's working on him and cannot come to the phone."

"Is he okay?"

"Well."

"Is he dead?!"

"He wants you to come to Bend, but to not come alone."

"Is he alive?"

"Yes, right now he is."

Within one second, our lives changed forever.

I never met a person whose life turned out exactly the way they planned. Life consists of breath-taking moments, anticipatory moments, enjoyable moments, perilous moments, and devastating moments. But in all those moments, God meets us where we are with exactly what we need.

> *"And this same God who takes care of me*
> *will supply all your needs from his glorious riches*
> *which have been given to us in Christ Jesus."*
> PHILIPPIANS 4:19 (NLT)

Let the beauty of that sink into your spirit. When our relationship with Christ is intimate, he supplies all we need. I was in desolate places where peace seemed nowhere to be found. God was always with me, even in the crazy, 'how am I going to do this?' times. He had not changed. He was always with me. Stand in the His light. Let Him meet you where you stand.

Tiny white paddles

Mom's mobility was changing. I searched for accessible outings for us. We decided to drive to a local boutique. You know the one: hand-dipped candles, unique stationary, and fun home décor. I held the door open and she pushed in her rolling walker, trying to maneuver the tight aisles.

In the middle of the store were free samples of a lush organic lavender lotion, along with small white paddles to apply the samples to the skin. While I was distracted by fragrant, wine-scented candles, Mom loaded a tiny white paddle with lotion.

She popped it into her mouth like candy. Instantly, she began sputtering and needed to spit. The storekeeper grabbed a napkin for her and I gave it to her just in time. I was aghast, my eyes bugged out.

"I thought it was jam!"

I'm so embarrassed. I can't believe she ate lotion. It's my favorite store, too, and I know everyone here.

"Are you okay Mom? It's about time for us to go, anyway."

"I'm fine. I saw those paddles and I thought it was something to eat!"

"Yes, I see why you did it." *I do not see how she thought it was edible!*

I realized she needed more attentiveness. Hindsight, I could have laughed when she ate the lavender lotion. My caregiver years were young and my toolbox was sparse. Instead, ugly pride rose up in me and shoved its way through the door. Funny stuff is bound to happen. Get ready to laugh. Kick ego out the door. Humility will become your good friend, and then grace arrives. And grace is always full of laughter.

Two grapes

Growing up, we were taught not to steal. Anything. My mom, Jim, and I were spending the summer at Rockaway Beach managing the Polyanna Motel we owned. Twelve cabins and fifty feet from the soft sand and ocean. Jim and I helped Mom clean cabins every morning. Our reward was running to the penny arcade to play pinball. After a few hours of pinball,

Jim—eleven years of age—and me—six years of age—walked across the street to the grocery store to buy the green grapes Mom needed.

While we were perusing grapes, Jim said, "Go ahead and try one to see if they taste good."

"No, we shouldn't"

"Oh, go on! It's okay. Try one to see I Mom will like them."

I ate two grapes.

"These are a good bunch of grapes. Mom will like these!"

He was satisfied and paid for the grapes with the money Mom had given him earlier. Immediately, Jim shot out of the store running home as fast as he could, leaving my six-year-old legs far behind. He raced into the motel office panting, "Mom! Kay Nell stole some grapes!" When I arrived several minutes behind him, Mom was waiting for me with hands on her hips.

"I'm disappointed in you. I cannot believe you stole grapes!"

She was so tall and made at me. I must be awful to do such a thing. I feel ashamed of myself and guilty. This was the only the second time I felt shame in my six years of living, and today the secondary feeling was guilt.

"I'm sorry, Mommy." Tears were flowing down my little red cheeks.

"Well, you know what you need to do. I'm taking you back and you will apologize to the store owner for stealing grapes. You will pay for the grapes from your allowance." She was determined.

It was the longest walk to the store. With my coins in hand, she reiterated exactly what I needed to say to the store owner, while she held my right hand.

"I'm sorry. I stole grapes. I'm so sorry. Here is the money for the grapes." I sheepishly looked in his eyes.

"Oh, you don't need to pay for them. I appreciate you telling me. How many grapes did you take?", said the grace-filled store owner.

"Two."

"Only two grapes?"

"Yes", wondering if they were going to put me in jail.

Mom insisted I pay. As we walked home, Mom questioned, "Why didn't you tell me you only ate two grapes?"

"You didn't ask. I felt so bad for eating two grapes." I hung my head.

Later, Mom told me she was surprised I was only eating two grapes to test the bunch. Jim had enjoyed baiting me and tattling that day, but thankfully, it wasn't his usual mode of operation. He must have been having a tough day as an eleven-year-old boy, too.

As I remember correctly, Mom and I walked by the ice cream store and came out with a big cones in our hands for the walk back home.

Lies versus truth

If I was free from caregiving, my life would be perfect. Entire days would be at home, exploring my new life after early retirement. I'm making every effort to nurture myself: exercising, praying, reading, and planning. I want to be the best woman, mom, daughter, sister and wife.

In the midst of my stinking thinking, wonderful things were still happening. One hot summer day, young Jordan and I created a table in our flower garden from old buckets that held an old door and two tablecloths on top. We were energized by our creativity. Two tiki torches set the mood, and we scattered rose petals on our new-to-us table in the cool of the evening. By the light of the tiki torches, we read books together in our new haven.

I was a caregiver for Mom because I chose it, and it was worth the steep price. I was frustrated many times; I was in my fourth decade, but frequently felt in my eighth decade. My lifeblood was sucked out of me with the unexpected phone calls, emergency hospital trips, and keeping her physically clean.

It was easier to give care if she lived with us. I left my family to travel to Mom's at a moment's notice; I was exhausted and frustrated.

It was a gouging out to grow in depth, wisdom, and experience. I seized opportunities to have crazy, silly fun with Jordan. We laughed and played together, carefree.

Eventually, I was heading to menopause like a trucker on the interstate; periodically suffering anxiety for the first time. This current season was the best time of my life, while the worst was happening with Mom. I didn't want to miss it: the caregiving, Jordan, and Phil. I made up stories in my mind of people walking by, how their lives were free-flowing, going where they wished carefree, easy, fun and perfect. What a waste of my time.

Truthfully, my life would not have been different if

I wasn't caregiving. I enjoyed helping others. Phil's parents were not in good health, and Mom was in fluctuating health. My brother, Jim, with Parkinson's disease diagnosed at forty-three years of age, was suffering daily from being sprayed multiple times with Agent Orange in Vietnam, as he served our country twenty-five years prior. Several of my beautiful nieces struggled with marital upheavals and chronic pain. They are all active believers, and living out their faith fearlessly.

God selected the perfect extended family for me and placed me within it. They are all believers. God did not make a mistake. He is not surprised. I love them all.

There are good things happening in caregiving. There are good things happening in our lives. I'm reminded of the song "Waymaker"[5]. Even when I don't see it or feel it, I know our God is actively working. He is actively working in your life, too.

He is always with you. He always provides for you. He always strengthens you. He always answers you. He always protects you. He always loves you. You are using your strength of mind and living out your faith fearlessly.

_____

5 "Waymaker" song, by Leland. https://youtu.be/iJCV_2H9xD0

Here & Now Reflection

ARE YOU WILLING?

"Hi, my mom is in the Emergency Room and the medic said to talk with the front desk person."

"Yes. I need a copy of her Medicare card, photo ID, supplemental insurance card, address, emergency contact, phone number, and medical history. "

And her first born.

"Thanks for the information, you can take a seat over there in the waiting room."

"No. I need to go into the Emergency Room with her."

"Oh, they're checking things out with her. You can wait here and they will come out after a while and take you back."

"No, my mom is unable to make decisions or speak for herself. I am her Health Care Representative, Power of Attorney, and her Advocate."

"Oh, okay." She buzzed me into ER.

A nurse arrived.

"Would you help me catheterize your mother? It'd be a lot easier."

No!

"Absolutely I'll help you."

The nurse schooled me, and it was clinically fascinating. I dug deep and learned how to be an intense caregiver, as the gates had swung wide open with physical boundaries shoved down the road. Mom had no mental or physical concept of what was happening. I was grateful.

"Kay Nell, I know you have a vacation planned. I'm going to be fine. Go ahead. Go be with your family. That's important. Go! I'll be fine."

Did I hear her right? God just opened a window inside her mind! A cool summer breeze blew in, without dementia present. My spirit is soaring. This is the mom I know! Exactly what she would have said to me, without dementia's frostiness icing her mind; urging me to enjoy my family. Oh, thank you, God! I can rest easier knowing her heart.

Mom was admitted to the hospital for pneumonia, as we left for our Central Oregon vacation. My brother's family stepped up to visit her in the hospital while we were gone.

On vacation, I called doctors twice a day for updates. Fun family memories and sad memories were comingling; a life balance I became intimate with in the years ahead.

My greatest fear while I was on vacation was her death. I didn't know if I could handle not being present when she passed. Trust came hard for me, but trusting God on this trip was only a warm up.

You may need to make tough judgment calls at some point. Honoring your care recipient and honoring those you deeply love and who love you is a fine balance. If you find yourself banging your head up against a wall in health care rules, like I did, talk their talk. You are an advocate for your care recipient when they cannot understand, cannot talk coherently, or cannot make decisions. Listen and advocate for your care recipient. You will have your own success stories to tell.

What are you willing to do for your care recipient?

What comfortable things do you enjoy doing for them?

When was the last time you were uncomfortable and did it anyway?

What did you learn about yourself during that time?

BREATHING DEEP

We pushed through the heavy door of Bonanza Café--
owners, Terry and Cheryl Platt. It was exactly like the
"Cheers" television show, everybody knew our names.
Our booth was to the left third booth in, next to a large
window with birds to watch. The early morning loggers
were in their booths guffawing over the latest timber stories and reviewing practical jokes they had played on
each other the day before.

Spirit knew I needed the ritual, the mornings, and
the evenings. Exhausted from twelve-to-fourteen-hour
work days, we shuffled up the rough concrete steps,
pulled back the heavily-worn door and were met with
tantalizing aromas and flames shooting up off the grill.
The owner, Cheryl, came by with water.

"Decaf coffee this morning. I'm already too wired!"

"You're not pregnant, are you?! You never get decaf!"

"Yeah, right. No way! I'm sure!"

*Why would she assume I'm pregnant?! We were married
eighteen years and people stopped asking. I ordered decaf coffee for
the first time. Shoot!*

"Congratulations!" Cheryl said several months later as she eagerly came to our table, wrestled our new baby boy, Jordan, from his carrier, and introduced him to others. Phil and I were enjoying our first hot meal in a months.

Audrey--in the fall of living--enjoyed a simple daily breakfast, played her lucky Keno numbers, and passed on Lincoln Logs for Jordan.

Soon Jordan will be coming up the rough steps on his own, pulling open the heavily-worn door, and be greeted by the waitstaff and regulars, and he will think he's home.

Familiar routines

This morning my routine was awaking about seven in the morning, grabbing an herbal tea, finding my home-made oat bran muffin, reading a devotional, and watching my favorite local television station for thirty minutes.

Creating familiar routines is one of the greatest pleasures in life. Even if you're not a person who likes routines, you still have them. Finding routines with your care recipient will be soothing to them, just as it is to you.

Junior High Jordan was home only ten minutes and we quarreled about something of no real consequence. There were relationships that needed tending at the same time as I was caregiving. Getting into the rhythm of a precious relationship and arriving home from a full day of caregiving challenges was exhausting and confusing. Caregiving was like playing my beloved classical music piece and in the next minute rocking out to some

head-banging music. The transitions were often missing. I needed familiar routines to outline my days.

I was driving home from a Waves of Mercy Christian
women's retreat event I'd planned. I needed time to
transition from the bliss of retreat back into caregiving.
How do you create those rhythms of transitions? What
if those relationships are a tad volatile already? What do
you do about it? It gets complicated sometimes, doesn't
it? Not so much the multiple tasks, but the multiple relationships we are actively nurturing along the way. How
can you find your way in relationships while a caregiver?

Core work

NASA reports the center core of our earth is iron with
a radius of 760 miles, surrounded by an outer core of
nickel-iron alloy, and is about 1,355 miles thick.[6] During
the 2020 pandemic, three friends and I worked on our
core in a private swimming pool, the major muscles
holding our bodies together.

Caregiving involves your core people, and you are
a team. Your support may be a paid caregiver, a chef,
housecleaner, nurse, or a medication disperser. As a
caregiver, the care recipient's family may or may not be
an integral part of your team.

There are unfamiliar paths for caregivers and care
recipients, when their health frequently changes. Toss
in familiar routines in simple ways. Go with your care
recipient to their favorite restaurant or treat them to

---

6 https://www.space.com/17777-what-is-earth-made-of.html

your favorite restaurant. It's a wonderfully cozy way to step into a familiar path, encouraging a positive, lighter routine. Grab a coffee and enjoy a moment by a wetland or lake with them.

Some said I wasted my time doing any kind of self-care. They had demands on me and didn't want me to change. They didn't understand the intensity of caregiving. It is of no consequence what others say about you during your caregiving time. You cannot control it, anyway.

Take alone time and you'll return with a renewed clarity about your life and the way you're living it. If changes are in order, make them. Kindness. Love above all. No one is coming to give you permission to take care of yourself. No one is coming to rescue you. It's up to you.

My friends at coffee were lamenting the need for a quiet moment in their lives. Our secret fantasy was buying a tiny house—a she-shed--and not allowing interruptions.

"I want a she-shed! There's no place in my home for me to get away!"

"Well, I go to the office, bedroom, family room or bathroom."

"Bathroom?"

"Yep. It's the only place no one will disturb me."

"No one is going to save us except ourselves for that alone time! We keep waiting for someone to give us permission, but no one is coming."

Revitalizing is a necessity as a caregiver. Give yourself permission.

How do you revitalize? Is it invigorating to chat with

friends? Do you talk with a stranger, and consider them your new best friend? You may be revitalized when you're with people. Not me. I revitalize with my close family members and alone time.

I facilitated a few Waves of Mercy/Christian women retreats, and I finally reserved a private room for myself. Oh! The joy! When there was excessive stimulation, I disappeared to my private room, lay across the bed in the quiet space and breathed. It only took thirty minutes, and I was ready to reconnect with others. Many think I am a strong extrovert, but I need time, space, silence, prayer, pen, paper, and my Bible to revitalize.

Listening

Let others manage their own lives. Let go of the "fix it" mode. Don't be a know-it-all; settle back and enjoy the relationship. Listen; paraphrase back what you heard someone say. Listen some more. They need you to listen. Listen to what they are not saying. Ask questions. Many times trusted friends/family want advice or opinions. Let them ask for it. It may take all you have, but let them ask you for it. For me, if I have enough time and space to think or talk it out, I know exactly what I need to do in a situation. You do, too.

Limit repeaters.

If you know a person who repeats the same problems every time you see them (because they intend to do nothing about it in reality) limit the relationship a bit. Offer to pray with them, and get out of the way to allow God to do His perfect work in them. You will be drained unless you take the relationship to the God level. God creates character within me and stretches me. Sometimes I don't enjoy the growth. How about you? What relationships are requiring the most growth lately?

Take a deep breath

Wherever you are--driving to caregiving, taking kids to practices, shopping, coffee with friends, or wrenching on a car--live in the moment. Be intentional. Take a deep breath and look at what and who is around you right now. The smells, the sounds. Stop thinking you are missing something and rushing wherever you go. Sounds like solid advice. It would be if I had always taken it. I still have trouble going to bed if anyone is still up because I'm afraid I'm going to miss out on something. Missing what? I have no idea. While taking naps something great might happen, and I'll have missed it.

At a deeper look, I trusted a completely good, good Father and I was in the right place at the right time, whether I was sleeping or awake. Listen to Him. He's not asleep. Dropping off to sleep during the day was not normally my go-to.

I've learned to nap intentionally sometimes. You cannot be caregiving and listening intently to your kids, spouse, or best friend and texting on your phone all at the same time. They know you're not present, but somewhere else in your mind. Gazing at the past and wishing things were different was a waste of my brain cells. Nothing was back there for me. Jumping into the future to the next carrot in my eyeballs was not living in the present.

Take a deep breath. Go on. Take it. Breathe deep. Exhale slowly and completely. Now look around you. Who or what is before you? If it's people, engage with them. If it's a task, put yourself into it, soaking up the present moment. Remember, people before tasks. Breathe.

Stress shows

Recently I had two teenagers help me prepare for a large, outdoor event at my home. They had one hour to give me. The first fifteen minutes they spent petting my cat, Blue.

Trying to get the task-ball rolling, I instructed the kind, young man.

"Okay, here's the pressure washer. Connect the hose in, go down the hill and turn on the water and get started."

The teen girl was still petting Blue. I barked orders.

"You get the chairs for him to pressure wash."

I could tell they had no idea.

"Okay, here's how you pressure wash a chair."

I'm lining up chairs to keep the pressure washing system going.

The girl looked at me, watched and announced to the boy.

"Wow, you're doing a great job!"

Seriously? You're moving at a snail's pace, more interested in chatting than getting the tasks done. The event is in a couple of days. There's so much to do. I needed to be in my recliner knowing they were doing the tasks. Yet, here I am, pushing both of them to get moving and get the job done. How can anyone not know how to pressure wash?! I gotta teach him. I'm exhausted and we're just getting started. And I'm in deep physical pain.

I felt like I was pushing against a thousand-pound weight to move them forward. The result was, I became highly task-oriented, in silent pain, and frustrated this wasn't going how I pictured. I made what could have been a rather pleasant day more intense, with a knife-sharp, task-only attitude, along with my high expectations.

I called them later and apologized for my harshness and intensity in accomplishing the tasks. They were gracious and forgave me. I could have told them I was in a lot of pain, then sat in a chair, and found joy while giving gentle instructions. I did not. The task was dominating. It was not my best moment.

Some of you may say you are task-oriented and don't need people. A lie. It's not all about you. Others may need your presence and enjoy your company, even in silence.

Dennis idolized Elvis Presley and shared details few people knew about him. Our Elvis conversations took place in the assisted-living facility's front lobby, next to a warm fireplace. He had the most Elvis memorabilia I had ever seen. Dennis was in his fifth decade and lived life from his power wheelchair, with cerebral palsy, his entire life. He rented an apartment on the ground floor with his mother, but she passed, so now it's Dennis who weaves in and out of my life. And Elvis.

If you are relentlessly task-oriented, you will miss out on some of the best parts of life. Tasks are endless. Your intensity alienates people from you. I know. I've done it. Allowing God, who loves you, to grow you beyond your shortsighted view, makes your life laser-focused, and satisfying. Loving people creates a humble, grace-filled life, with a large dose of patience. Stress shows. Love heals.

Here & Now Reflection

SELF-CARE

What are you experiencing today? Are you on top of the world? Lower than a worm? Are you looking at what is in front of you? Some days seem perfect; everything is going seamlessly. The care recipient is doing well and content. It's a good day. The lower-than-a-worm days are rough. Nothing goes right. Advocating is troublesome, and no one is cooperating.

Try not to judge your day of caregiving. There's no need to put extra pressure on yourself. I know you're doing your best. When you're having a tough day caregiving, take time to do what makes you truly happy.

Meet up with a good friend. You know--the friend who is easy to be around, and cares about you whether you are up or down. Such a beautiful flow in those relationships. If you don't have one, keep searching until you find a loyal friendship. It's worth it, and will bolster you to gently keep pushing forward.

When is the last time you took time to connect with your close friend, a mentor, or a life coach?

Do you procrastinate self-care, and if so, what does good self-care look like to you?

Name two friends you will contact in the next couple of days.

MULTIPLYING
HOPE

"Can't we skip church today and just go straight to the car destruction derby, Dad?"

"We're going to early church as a family and we'll go after that."

"Ah, c'mon! We'll be fine to skip it."

"No. We're going to worship God with our church family. We won't miss a moment of the car destruction derby. I promise."

There's an explosion of religions around the world. In New Guinea, some worship giant yams. In India, some worship motorcycles. Messianic Jews are believers and waiting for Jesus to return. In Kansas, some worship a flying spaghetti monster. Christians worship God and believe Jesus is the Christ, the Son of the living God who is full of grace, mercy, and love towards every single person in the world.

Dogmatic opinions

Acquaint yourself with the care recipient's spiritual life. You may need to help with their religious practice. Put aside your desire to persuade, if you do not agree with their belief system. You have the opportunity to offer them grace, mercy, love, peace, and the freedom to pursue their deep beliefs. If you cannot help them, it is best you ask another to fill the role, and keep any dogmatic opinions to yourself. If they ask about your faith walk, welcome the visit. A healthy spiritual life can be one of great inner peace, freedom and unity.

My spiritual life is not believing "in" God, Jesus, the Holy Spirit; but truly taking the time to know Him on a deep, personal level--a relationship. However, I know not everyone in the world believes the way I do. I can still show great love, respect, and compassion for a care recipient who thinks differently.

What are your beliefs as a caregiver? Are your beliefs including or alienating? Do you believe strongly about your spiritual life or are you unsure about even creating one? As a caregiver, think about your own beliefs, values, and purpose and how it affects your caregiving style. Strong opinions are just that. Opinions. You do not need to insist your care recipient thinks exactly like you do. Open dialogue only happens in an atmosphere of love.

Hope Multiplies

Part of a vital spiritual life encompasses hope. Is your care recipient hopeful? Why or why not? Do you exercise a hopeful attitude? You may be coming into a less-than-ideal situation with a care recipient. If you are feeling depressed, this is probably not the best time to give care. Hope never disappoints us. It is a basic human need to hope. Hope is linked to a vital spiritual life and a joy-filled courageous attitude. If you are full of hope, how may you inspire your care recipient to become full of hope today, too? Hope multiplies when it is shared.

God's sovereignty

Where is faith in God in the midst of suffering? Mom's second husband was dying of cancer. Hospice was called. One or two days and he'd be in His presence. My beliefs felt shaky at twenty-nine years old.

Why doesn't God heal him? Where is God in the midst of watching this tremendous suffering? I've prayed and prayed and prayed. Still. He suffers.

I was learning a life lesson about letting go and God's sovereignty. Someone close to my heart was intensely suffering. His body was wasting away. God, full of grace, was teaching me slowly and gently; trusting Him was my part. Faith is never wasted. God loves when we move in faith with Him, counting on Him, depending on Him.

> *"Your kingdom come. Your will be done on earth as it is in heaven."*
> MATTHEW 6:10 (CSB)

And, although my will would never have him die, over the years I accepted His will even when I didn't understand it.

Grief bubbling up

Tears fell out of Mom's eyes.

"I'm done grieving."

Grief is a gift. Grief often comes bubbling up at inopportune moments. You can choose to heal or postpone the healing. Accept the healing. If we choose to deny the healing, isolation, anger, and depression will come to camp out.

If your care recipient had memory loss, your grief slipped in and lingered constantly, saying good-byes day after day. Allow yourself to grieve frequently, seldom, alone, or with a close friend. There's no timeframe or perfect way to grieve. Abstain from excesses while grieving as it inadequately postpones emotional pain and when the effect wears away, the grief will still be there to travel through. Grief comes in unexpected ways, unique to your personality. Grace yourself with grieving as long as it takes. No judging. No expectations. Put one foot in front of the other each day. Grieving tears are healing. It took me a long time to accept this. Every time grieving arrives and tears flow, you can be sure healing is on its heels.

My grieving process lasted a long time with my mom, due to her slowly progressing vascular dementia. Closing the door to her apartment each day, tears often rolled down my cheeks. I was never in denial. It was crystal-clear where Mom and I were traveling. The grieving was in the daily; the sadness always in the background of everything I did. No one noticed it, except Phil, God, and me.

Recently, three of my friends died within thirty days. One, a forty-four-year-old man—George--a next-door neighbor for many years. Too young to die leaving a wife, young children, brother, and his parents behind. I sent his mother a note, without clichés or silly phrases. I just said how very sorry I was she was experiencing such pain, we were praying, and he was a good man. No words sufficed, but you must reach out.

Another God-centered, encouraging, passionate seventy-year-old woman took her own life. I went by the next day to bring food, hug on her family, and listen. No one saw it coming. She'd written a note to me and several others two days prior, without a hint. Family, friends, and a delightful grandson were left strewn to negotiate their rocky, swampy path filled days with many holes.

The third loss was a sixty-five year old friend from grade school through high school. I went to see Ben's mother as soon as I heard. She held onto me, weeping.

"I'm so sorry you are experiencing this pain. There are really no words."

"You're right. There are no words for this loss. He called or came to see me every day. I don't know what I'll do now."

"Wow. What a gift that was. I've watched you. You will move forward and depend on your older son. He needs you. He will try to be strong for you, but he is grieving, too."

"Yes. He's a good son. I know. Ben's son is marrying in two days at their family home. My grandson was going to cancel his wedding, but I told him, your dad would want you to have the wedding there."

"Yes. He would."

Then she walked into my arms again, weeping for a bit. No words.

She called after me, "You come by anytime to see me!"

Climbing into my car, I was grateful my mom taught me well when others experienced tragedy. Please don't stay away. Bring food, a card, memorial dollars, or just yourself. Don't agonize what to say. There's truly nothing to be said except to listen.

There were no funerals due to COVID-19 in our area. Businesses, churches, stores and restaurants were closed. There was only quarantine. I've grieved many times, but sometimes grief is so large I know I cannot carry it. I give my losses over and over again to God. In my mind, I am taking my hands and pushing them onto Jesus. He's the only one who can handle some dark grief. Just let me say, "I hate death".

"Death and Hades were thrown into the lake of fire.
This is the second death, the lake of fire.
REVELATION 20:14 (CSB)

He will wipe away ever tear from their eyes. Death will
no longer exist; grief, crying, and pain will exist no longer,
because the previous things have passed away.
REVELATION 21:4 (CSB)

I will spin around, dance, and yell in victory when death is defeated. But until then, I must keep moving forward. So do you.

Phil and I enjoyed putting together 1,000-piece puzzles on our roomy dining room table, always leaving enough room to play a card game, if it presented itself. We saw how the puzzle looked from the photo on the box or from a large blow-up photo inside the box. We found the side pieces first. We had no idea where ninety-five percent of the other pieces were to be placed.

I had a piece of the puzzle, but God saw the completed puzzle. When I step into heaven, see Him face to face, I will understand completely. Our family had a tiny piece of the puzzle of my mom's second husband's life. I was learning to trust God with the rest. Not a one-time lesson for me. A couple days later, her husband stepped right into heaven, more alive than he ever was. We were still living our lives here without him, though. Grief bubbles up.

Faith walks

Caregiving for Mom was the biggest challenge of my life. Nurturing a personal relationship with Jesus made a massive difference in my coping abilities. Caregiving refined my character, taught me patience, created hope, and required endurance. Boldness and humility came from spending time with Jesus. Why act shy when God played a major role in keeping me functioning well as a woman, a caregiver, a wife, and a mom. Show some spunk! Pray alone (or with sisters-in-Christ) study your Bible, and apply truth to your daily life.

Looking at cars was easy; buying a car was easy; washing a car was easy; polishing a car was easy; but driving a car took practice, practice, practice. You grew into driving by putting in the hours. It's the same in your faith walk. You're growing, not going for perfection; following Him until one day you see Him face-to-face and understand everything that confounds you now.

God gave me purpose. Concrete purpose. I remained unchanged about God, no matter what went on around me, no matter what anyone said, no matter what came in close and attempted to darken my path. I have a myriad of questions, but my faith walk gives me unchanging hope, grace, mercy, love, and the challenge of extending it to others.

You know the ones. The push-my-button, sarcastic, and hurtful ones. They are suffering, and the ones you are to extend the most hope, grace, mercy, and love. After all, He did it for me even though He knew all the messes I have made. He loves me. He loves you. Courage and forgiveness are a necessity for the trip. Faith will be walking along with them.

Living with intention

Who was I anymore, apart from caregiving? My family and I went on a week vacation, and I didn't call Mom once. Family was visiting her often. Slowly, as the week passed, I discovered who I was again. I didn't neglect the caregiving God called me to, but I began doing it more intentionally. I was stuck in some negative intentions of guilt, checklists, no boundaries, and duty above all.

What are your intentions as you prepare to care-give? What are your intentions for going away for a week or more? Will you return refreshed as a caregiver?

God brought me clarity, intentional direction, concrete guidance, and His peace as I sought Him. It didn't happen overnight. Phil and I did yoga for years. Yoga didn't do it. A six-week Mindfulness Stress Reduction class didn't do it. The classes were excellent. They gave me resources to breathe and relax. They didn't lead me to true hope, truth, and life. Only God. Him alone.

There were times I've played God. It was devastatingly exhausting in the end. We tried teaching Jordan tools to cope with life as it came. As a child and adult, he frequently had more clarity, more direction, more forgiveness, more concrete guidance, and more love than I dreamed. Above all, love and forgive. You are fearless and full of hope.

Here & Now Reflection

INTENTION

In this chapter, we talked about opinions, hope, grief, faith, and intention.

What are you willing to commit to in your spiritual life? What are you willing to let go and accept opinions differing from yours?

Jot down a time you were hopeless and a time you were full of hope.

When was the last time you allowed yourself to cry as a caregiver?

Jot down the top three times your faith has grown in the last two years.

Who are you challenged to forgive? Remember, you can still forgive even if the other person does not and even if you have no idea why they are unforgiving. Will you forgive them today, tomorrow, and the next day. Forgiveness is a process, like peeling an onion. It may make you cry, but it will be good once it is done each time.

LIGHTNING STRIKES

My dad went into heaven two years prior. Our family needed an adventure and new memories to draw us together, the ones who were left behind. My humorous brother, Jim; his perky, encouraging wife, Cheryl; my three-year-old and one-year-old nieces, Heidi and Heather; and my patient husband, Phil, and I were ready for a fun vacation and some good family bonding.

Road-worthy

A friend, Andrea, generously loaned us her Class A motorhome. Finally, the day came to leave our jobs behind and begin our trip. The morning we were to leave, Andrea's motorhome broke down before we laid eyes on it. It was not road-worthy.

Maybe God doesn't want us to go.

Goose egg

Another friend, Bob, offered to loan us his Class A motorhome.

"The trip is back on! Vacation, here we come!"

God, you must want us to take this motorhome. Thank you!

Phil and Jim were experienced with riding dirt bike motorcycles, driving camping trailers, and maneuvering large vans for their carpet-laying business.

"How hard could driving this motorhome really be? It'll be a cinch."

We all met at Jim and Cheryl's country home and packed plenty of food, clothes, shoes, toys, diapers and pull-ups for the littles. We were Nebraska-bound for a much needed visit with relatives.

Cheryl and the little girls sat securely on the horseshoe round bench surrounding the built-in table. Mom was an energetic sixty-five year old, standing up in the aisle at the back, organizing things. Jim elected Phil to drive the motorhome first, with Jim in the passenger seat. Phil gently shifted into reverse to get into the right direction to exit the driveway. Backing up was going excellently. Phil was a pro, until he stomped on the brakes and screeched to a dead stop. Mom flew like a roadrunner bird down the aisle, with a gash and a goose egg bump on her head.

Phil shifted the motorhome beast into park, and we gathered around Mom, encouraging her to lay down and relax. Loving Cheryl brought an ice pack from the refrigerator and made a good compress for Mom's head. The gash wasn't deep, and the goose egg would eventually discolor and shrink. As only a three-year-old could do, Heidi comforted her grandma, lying down with her. Once we gave mom tender loving care, we knew she would recover quickly. She was resilient and always ready for adventure.

Again, we walked to our respective positions. Phil started the engine, backed up again. This time he slowly, gently applied the brake, and we coasted to an easy, smooth stop. He made the right turn onto the highway and away we went.

It was almost twenty-five minutes before the motorhome coughed, sputtered and came to a halt on the side of a busy freeway. Phil and Jim grabbed their tools, exited the door and propped open the hood. From inside the motorhome, we heard banging, twisting, and short, amiable discussions outside. In fifteen minutes, Phil and Jim were back inside and we were heading down the freeway. Everyone was grateful they fixed it.

We roamed the motorhome cabin, listened to the little girls chatter away, and were hopeful. Mom loved them deeply. Five hours we sailed smoothly down the road. The motorhome once again coughed, sputtered and came to a halt on the side of the freeway about an hour from the nearest town: Baker City, Oregon.

Jim and Phil grabbed the tools again. Jim grumbled as they stepped out the door; propped up the hood, and more discussions.

God's got this

This was where my mom's personality shined. She was fearless. Years earlier, flying to Fallon, Nevada, to the burial of her second husband, she was not deterred when lightning crashed onto the wing of our airplane.

"Oh! Isn't that beautiful? Such bright lights!"

"Mom, that's lightning! That's not good."

"Oh, Kay Nell, there's nothing you can do about it. You may as well enjoy it. The pilots know what they are doing. God's got this."

I gripped the armrests tighter. *I'm not sure He does.*

Snippy teenagers

When I was a snippy, rolling my eyes fifteen-year-old, I sauntered into the kitchen, plopped myself down to my awaiting breakfast Mom had meticulously prepared. One-half grapefruit with each section precut, and Cheerios with powdered skim milk. Mom always sat at the table quietly reading her Bible, and I knew she'd been praying. This morning, she was grinning like she knew something I didn't.

"What now, Mom?"

"Oh, Kay Nell, this scripture is so exciting! It's just amazing."

"Okay, what scripture?"

"Listen to this! It's going to be so exciting! We meet the Lord in the air! It says it here!"

> *"For the Lord Himself will descend from heaven with a shout, with the archangel's voice, and with the trumpet of God and the dead in Christ will rise first. Then we who are still alive will be caught up together with them in the clouds to meet the Lord in the air and so we will always be with the Lord."*
> 1 THESSALONIANS 4:16-17 (CSB)

"Yeah, I guess that's cool."

I remember the morning like it was yesterday. If you

get eye rolling and apathy, take heart; God's word goes out and accomplishes its purpose. His word is powerful. Inside I was wide-eyed excited to meet the Lord in the air!

This would be a great day to meet the Lord in the air and out of this vacation!

"Let's have breakfast! We're stopped and it may be a while before this motorhome is fixed. I'll cook breakfast."

Is she crazy? It's my mom's superpower—making something bad into something fun. I still find it annoying. How does she do it? Doesn't she see we're stuck on a freeway, with no traffic, in the middle of nowhere?!

"I think I'll make eggs, bacon, hash browns, toast, and coffee. Doesn't it sound good?"

My sister-in-love, Cheryl, chimed in enthusiastically. She and mom were cut from the same cloth.

"Yes! Sounds fantastic! What a wonderful idea."

"Yay grandma! Let me help! I want to crack the eggs! Pleeeeese?"

Who are these people? Don't they know we haven't even left Oregon?!

"Son of a gun outfit!" Jim grumbled and repeated what we heard our dad say many times in exasperation, as he stomped into the motorhome.

Thumb Sucking

"The motorhome is completely shot. Gonna have to call a tow truck. Maybe the motorhome just needs a little tweaking and the local mechanic will fix it, and we'll be back on the road in no time."

I don't understand this, God. I thought you wanted us to go on this trip.

"Yeah, we're out here on the freeway broke down with our motorhome. We need to be towed. Can you come and tow us into Baker City to a good mechanic there?"

Just as we finished a hearty two-hour breakfast, a grumpy tow-truck man arrived. He pulled up in front of the motorhome, edged backwards, and connected the towing equipment. The tow-truck sat one person and my brother was elected. The six of us were seated like sardines at the horseshoe table. The tow-truck driver veered a sharp left, and punched the gas--like he was in a demolition derby-- into an extra-wide median between the highways.

"Aaaaaaaaaaaaah!"

We all protected Heidi and Heather. The motorhome veered up on two left wheels, bounced down hard, then up onto the two right wheels, crashed down on all four wheels as he finally hit pavement and headed back to Baker City.

"Hmmmm." The lone mechanic gazed under the hood and shook his head.

"Hmmmm. No one can look at this motorhome for a week, and I'm not sure I can fix it then."

The three-year-old and one-year-old were exhausted and cried--one sucking her thumb and one sucking her index finger.

"What?! We'll pay anything! There's no way we can stay here for a week waiting for a motorhome you might be able to fix." Jim showed his desperation.

"No one can look at this motorhome for a week, sir."

Jim, Phil, and I loaded up six black as coal garbage bags full of our belongings. Poor Cheryl was riding herd and consoling the confused, weary little girls, who were still sucking their thumb and index finger.

I highly considered the thumb-sucking option.

The cold-hearted mechanic pointed to the Greyhound bus station about eight blocks away. We each carried two huge bags, but by the fourth block I was lifting and plopping, lifting and plopping my bags. Cheryl was gently shuffling the three-year-old and carrying the one-year-old. We looked like Ma and Pa Kettle in the city, carrying our belongings in black trash bags into the Greyhound Station.

Last time I rode a Greyhound bus, I was fifteen years of age, traveling Portland to El Paso to meet four hundred teenagers for an eight-week adventure at the Colégio Escuela de Torreón, México. The Greyhound bus looked the same.

Baker City people stared and stepped away from our troop. We didn't care. We knew how ridiculous we looked, but after Mom's head gash, two roadside wrenching escapades, a long wait for help on the side of the highway, a tow-truck guy nearly flipping the motorhome, and non-stop crying of the littles, Mom's breakfast was our sweetest memory.

We bought our bus tickets, while the bus driver shoved the trash bags into the storage underneath the bus. He looked back at us with a judging eye. We didn't care. The bus had seats for two, row after row. We filed in, grabbing the seats right behind each other. Jim and Cheryl had the three-year-old, Heidi, on their lap. Mom was in the last row, completely entertaining her one-year-old granddaughter, Heather. Phil and I were seated behind Mom and Heather. Sitting down was such a relief after our long walk.

Going home was the best option. We were anxious to walk into our relaxing homes, which only eight hours ago we couldn't wait to leave. As the Greyhound bus pulled out of the station, the rain began pouring and the wind blew. The bus driver was sitting forward on his cushy driver's seat, peering out the front window. The wipers were swishing back and forth at high speed, when all of a sudden one of the wipers came to a halt. It severely limited his view of the road. The five of us looked at each other, shook our heads and smiled a bit, as this was apropos for our family trip up to this point. We were confident things would get better. We were Christians and prayed several times during the trip for God's help, guidance, and blessings. The downpour, with limited vision, continued for the next five hours into Portland.

Once we were home, we began calling each other on our landline phones--mobile phones were not on the scene yet.

God's final plan
"We wish we could fly to Nebraska, but we don't have the money." Jim moaned.

"It's Saturday and I can't get into the bank to draw

out my money." Mom was disappointed she couldn't fix the problem.

Phil offered. "We have the cash. You wanna go? You can pay us back when we get home. Let's do it. Let's fly there together!"

"What? You have cash at home?!"

"Jim, ya wanna go or not? Get ready. I'll call for the flights. Get packed in suitcases this time."

"Okay, let's do it!"

At the Portland Airport, we walked up to the United Airlines counter and counted out cash for the seven of us.

"Why do you have all this cash?"

"Well, we were going to travel by motorhome, but two of them broke down and…"

"I see. Okay. Here are your tickets." As we walked a quarter-mile down the concourse, we noticed they ticketed my husband, Phil, as "Bill Boyd". The flight attendants didn't ask and we didn't tell. We were grateful for an uneventful flight. Our seats were across from each other; Jim and Cheryl and girls together, and Mom was across from Phil and I. About half way to Nebraska, an irate man turned to his right and yelled directly at three-year-old Heidi.

"Shut up! Stop kicking my seat! You need to stop it! Stop kicking my seat, little girl!"

Jim shot up and yelled.

"Don't you ever talk to my daughter that way! You got a problem, you talk to me! You need to settle down, or I'll beat the crap out of you."

Phil and I tried to look away from the train wreck.

The man huffily plopped back down, but I could smell fear in him. He had rattled the cage. Jim was wound a little tight. He was on edge and in no mood to allow a stranger to scream at his daughter. The rest of the flight was quiet.

After we landed in Denver, we boarded a puddle-jumper propeller plane to North Platte, Nebraska. About thirty people were aboard; twenty-three began throwing up in the aisle when the plane's air conditioning went out on that hot summer day. The stewardesses grabbed blankets and placed them in the aisle on top of the...well, you know. The seven of us resisted the urge, but Cheryl had a strong gag reflex, and it was all she could do to maintain decorum. We were so proud of her. The smell on the plane was worse than a dead skunk lying in the middle of the road in the heat. We finally landed, sweaty and woozy.

A silver lining was Cheryl's relative knew Mom's brother extremely well, even though they lived many miles apart, they had done some horse trading years before. Isn't it amazing how God gave this miracle of continuity and familiarity?

Without a glitch, Phil and I traveled by rental car to Kansas, visiting his sister, Carolyn. Her family was fun and our highlight was touring her husband's job in an AT&T underground facility, with a red room and red phone. We felt like spies. The rest of the trip was delightful.

Best made plans

This true story reminds me we could still be in the will of God, even when plans take twists and turns. It took tremendous perseverance, endurance, trust, and patience. He was building character in each of us, and He was with us the entire vacation. Caregiving requires using all of these tools, especially when you feel like you are alongside a desolate road, all alone.

Family road trips are worth every minute. Mom had the right idea, making joyful moments alongside the road in the midst of despair and exasperation.

Look around and find joy when your caregiving world may become dark and hopeless. After ten days, we safely arrived back home. Caregiving darkness is only for a small season. It will lift. I would be a caregiver for my mom all over again. I would even take that motorhome road trip again!

Here & Now Reflection

MEDITATING

You just read about a vacation starting out as a fiasco and ending with fun and joy. A few of us mumbled some when things weren't going as planned. Did you mumble to yourself recently?

Mumbling to yourself needs to be gentle, loving, truthful, and something you would say to a close friend. Meditating is great for your mental health, too. Please take the time to answer the following questions.

What situation has tested your faith when things didn't go as planned?

What do you need to meditate upon or preach to yourself today?

What parts of your story no longer serve you?

What stories are you attached to that you need to let go?

BELIEVING BETTER

My parents introduced me into a personal relationship with Jesus Christ that has permeated my entire life. By five years old I knew Jesus was my best friend and I would never leave Him. I held onto Him during the tumultuous years ahead. No one could take Him from me. Mom poured out her life for me in countless, selfless ways, always putting my needs first.

I desperately called Mom from my first-grade classroom, frantic the green paper dinosaur costume my classmates and I had designed wasn't working.

"Don't worry, my mom will come right away and help."

She did. She helped us make an authentic green dinosaur.

She was always game to do crazy things: learned to ride a bicycle at fifty years of age, jumped on a trampoline (nearly breaking her neck), threw a baseball to me for hours, taught me what she knew about piano, and loved me through my junior high years, when I thought she was incredibly stupid and rolled my eyes at her behind her back.

I learned who she really was when I was a sassy thirteen-year-old and my dad was at work, so I was extra sassy.

"Mom, you can't tell me what to do! You don't know anything!"

"Don't you talk that way to me Kay Nell! I can take you to the ground."

"Yeah. Right…"

I was on my back on the floor and she was on top of me.

"See? I may be shorter, but I'm feistier. Don't you ever talk that way to me again."

"Okay, okay. I get it. I didn't think you had it in you."

Up through my teen years, I loved her because she was my mom. She made things happen, and ran my universe.

In my twenties, I loved her because suddenly she was full of wisdom and the air I breathed.

In my thirties, I loved her by becoming, like her, an independent businesswoman, and loved her as a friend.

In my late forties, I showed my love for her in different ways. I laid out her clothes, scheduled her appointments, showered her, dressed her, and paid her bills. I was her memory. I never left her presence without an "I love you" and a light kiss on the cheek or forehead.

She relinquished running my universe, but she was still the air I breathed and a close friend. I was honored she escorted me through my forty-three years. Now I was honored to escort her through the final wintery thirteen years of her life.

She has been gone from my sight now for over ten years, and my dad has been out of view for nearly forty-five years, yet they are present with me. They taught me at an early age their beliefs, convictions, and values. I passed along many of them, the best I could, to Jordan.

Beliefs

Greek is pisteuo: to think to be true, to be persuaded of, to place confidence in

What have you accepted as truth?

What are you completely persuaded about?

Where is your confidence placed?

How have your beliefs enhanced your caregiving?

Convictions

Greek is élegxos: a proof, a test, an inner persuasion

What are you convinced about?

What thoughts challenged you now?

In what ways have you been tested in life?

How have your convictions enhanced your caregiving?

Values

Greek is misthapodotés: paying what is due, a rewarder, giving rewards in keeping with own values

What have you paid dearly for in your life?

How have you rewarded yourself?

How did your values line up with what you care about most?

How have these values enhanced your caregiving?

Please answer all the above questions. It's worth the work.

Time was created for people to mark off days, years, and seasons. We have an allotted time here on earth. Beliefs, convictions, and values are at your core. The beauty is found in making needed changes in one or more of these areas. You were unflinchingly brave and persevering as you assessed your beliefs, convictions, and values. All the work is worth it.

Accept help

Challenges are often a matter of resources and implementing them. If one resource path isn't a good fit, go to another resource, and try again.

You could hire a salon person to come in for hair, manicures and pedicures for your care recipient. With Mom, I chose to do the pedicures/manicures myself. She enjoyed them when her living had become small.

A friend, Patty, volunteered and we washed Mom's hair. Did it take time? Yes. Lots of time. But the look on Mom's face when we washed her hair was worth it all. A humble friend gave their time. Your friends may offer to help, too. Let them. Do not let your ego get in the way. Accept help. Extend gratitude.

Laundry is offered in an assisted-living facility. Write your care recipient's initials in all their clothes, towels, sheets, or anything washed. Get a small laundry roller cart to gather the dirty laundry for the facility to use. You also have the option to process their laundry yourself at the facility.

You may need to schedule their meals. Do it at the

same time each day, adding a cohesiveness to the day. Ritual. We all thrive on it. Is your care recipient more alert in the morning or the evening? Schedule the more difficult tasks or fun outings when they are the most alert. Schedule your peak caregiving hours when you are most alert, if possible.

Make your caregiver career, for however long, the easiest possible for those around you, but especially for yourself. No one wants a burned-out, grouchy, exhausted caregiver. Ask yourself what you would want if the tables were turned. What would you enjoy and how would it be done if you switched places with your care recipient? When things get a little foggy in what is best to do, ask yourself probing questions. Your answers will bring you clarity.

Caregiving flow

Flow is a deep focus on nothing but the present activity; not even your own self or emotions. Flow is running a race, creating music, or playing on the floor with a child.

A 2004 TED talk, by Csikszentmihalyi,[7] stated one's mind can attend to only a certain amount of information at a time; about 110 bits of information per second. It may sound like a lot of information, but simple daily tasks use up most of the information. Decoding speech, for instance, takes about sixty bits of information per second. When having a conversation, focused attention on other things does not create flow; living in the present moment does.

---

7 https://www.youtube.com/watch?v=I_u-Eh3h7Mo

The flow of caregiving is peaked when your care recipient presents a need and you respond with compassion and joy. It's a beautiful dance to watch flow between people. I've experienced it with Phil, Jordan, Nicole, and a few close friends. Where have you experienced flow?

Is your flow depending on others and what they do, don't do, or say? Flow was shelved then. This is no time for inflated ego, an "I'm too good for this job." Flow is killed. No joy. No bliss. No flow. When you were in the flow, energized, humbled, and joy-filled, laughter fast approaches.

Here & Now Reflection

RESPECT

Beliefs. Convictions. Values. You just answered several questions in this chapter about these qualities.

Honor your care recipient for living and surviving life this far. Give your care recipient respect and don't judge if they are worthy of it. If they cannot make decisions, let them pick between two things. Respect their choice. If they want you to choose, they made a decision.

Do something out of your comfort zone. Your care recipient is out of their comfort zone. This was not how they pictured their life and neither did you.

What help are you willing to receive this week? From whom?

How could you connect with your care recipient on a deeper level?

What will you do this week to step out of your comfort zone?

CHOOSING
VITALITY

Aging in Place

In 2020, some friends and I enjoyed an advanced water aerobics class at a private pool three days a week. Sometimes, when I drove to the store on the other two days, I was on automatic. I'd turn left towards the pool instead of going straight on the road to the store. Habits make strong connections in our brains and connect familiar places, routines, events, and emotions.

Imagine moving your care recipient after they established routines for years in their homes--memorable holidays and birthdays. They drove into their driveway and parked in the exact same spot, year after year. They walked in dimmed light to the bathroom in the middle of the night because they knew where obstacles were, and they maneuvered around them without even thinking.

The most vibrant living is by aging in place: continuity with familiar places and routine rituals. Friends and family are more eager to visit the care receiver's home, rather than a facility.

I've moved eight times within a fifteen-mile radius in the past sixty-six years. Each move required new routines, a settling in, and awkwardness for friends and family in the new surroundings for a while. We were at our previous home seventeen years, fourteen miles past our new home. We flew right past our new home more than once, heading out of town to our old place solely due to routines and habits.

Aging in place is a strong, viable solution for care recipients who need gradually more care, and it is the most economical. Think outside the box. Most care recipients would rather stay in their own home with increased care levels than move to a strange place. They may not know anyone there, and they would be living with solely elderly people.

Western culture has frequently placed their elderly parents in a facility. Many other cultures moved their parents into their own home and they became a family unit. This living provided increased mental, emotional, and physical health.

If a care recipient moved in with your family, create a space for their mental health--and yours. A separate no-step entrance, an accessible bed, 23"to 25" high, a small living room, and basic kitchen makes great studio living. Add a no-step-in shower and space to roll up to the sink, in case a wheelchair is in their future. These are simple, low-cost solutions to help it be a positive experience for everyone in the family. Caregivers, food preparation, and house cleaners may be needed at some point. It may seem like a more expensive way to go. It is not. Family living or care recipients who stayed in their own home was the least expensive route.

A friend of ours decided to stay in his home and hired paid caregivers to help with his breakfasts and some cleaning. He is the most curious ninety-six-year-old gentleman I've ever met. He is open to learning, asks intriguing questions, with a good sense of humor. Routines are in everything he does and it creates a strong sense of security for him. With a large family, he enjoys visitors for dinner several times a week. They bring the food, and he loves their company. Does he act happy every single day? Of course not. Neither do we. He chose to stay in his beloved, familiar home, and he is stronger because of it.

Assisted-Living Facilities

My mom married the third time, and they were encouraged by his family to move into a facility. Our family wanted her and her husband to stay in their home, come to live with us, or we could move into their home's basement, as it accommodated separate living space. With two families involved, the decisions became more complex. They eventually moved into an apartment in a facility, where they moved to the assisted-living side of the same facility, as their service needs increased.

Family members may split the expenses if the care recipient cannot pay their way. If you are a member of the care recipient's family, ask your family if they would like to participate in expenses. It is not your responsibility to make their decisions. Decide before you make calls to your family that it is their choice, and you're giving them opportunity to participate with you monetarily on behalf of your care recipient. If they do participate, please demonstrate integrity by keeping detailed financial records of expenses and income. You will want to be above reproach in this area; even if no one looks at the records, keep them. Be transparent.

Assisted-living facilities are enhanced by the extra services provided. These could include paid caregivers, medications given, housecleaners, transportation, or fun activities for each resident. The living choices are studio apartments, one-or two-bedroom apartments, including a small kitchen. Balconies on the upper floor units or a private entry with a porch are especially useful. If a porch entry is available, friends and family can enter their apartment from the outside and not enter through lobby doors and walking down halls. A porch or balcony is perfect for flowers, growing plants, and feeding birds, too.

A registered nurse (RN) is available twenty-four hours, seven days a week. Care recipient meetings are scheduled every three months and include interested family members. If the family does not come, the staff still meets. I highly recommend attending the meetings. Full three meals and desserts are prepared and served in the dining room with a specific table assigned, usually with three other diners. Happy hour, fresh cookies, and root beer floats are often served in the afternoon. Activities (painting, book club, exercise) and outings are planned most days. Outings may include casino trips, grocery shopping, mall shopping, and sightseeing excursions.

Paid caregivers enter your care recipient's room to

meet the needs they cannot do for themselves. Mom eventually had dementia and was in bed often, upon entering assisted living. I negotiated with the administration for paid caregivers to enter Mom's room, assess and meet her needs, and log in a notebook in her room every two hours. My strongest negotiating moments were during the initial admission process. Facilities promise much to secure a new resident, whether on Medicaid, or a personal pay. Insist everything be written and signed by the care recipient, family member, and the administrator.

Ask questions

What is the level of care? The goal is usually not move the care recipient again. If dementia is present, moving causes alarming stressors for the care recipient and their family.

What activities are available?

Will they enjoy what is offered?

How many caregivers per resident are on staff during the day, and how many on night shift? What are their first names?

Is a nursing supervisor on shift at night? Often facilities have fewer caregivers at night, and without a supervisor on site. Visiting Mom randomly in the middle of the night, I found staff watching TV, sleeping, no basic care met, outside smoking, or nowhere to be found. I'm not saying all facilities are the same at night, but after thirteen years of nightly visits, I assure you it is worth some unplanned visits.

Is there transportation for medical appointments or visiting people locally? How often is it available? How do they sign up to go? Will they come to their room to help them go, or do they need to be at the bus at a specific time on their own?

How much notice is needed for medical appointments? How long do they wait to be picked up from appointments?

Will they take food to the resident's apartment if needed?

Will they feed them if they become unable?

Elder abuse

A caveat – if you suspect elder abuse, the local Department of Aging thoroughly investigates all complaints on a case-by-case basis. All complaints and results are available to the public in the records stored at the Department of Aging. Before selecting a facility, research these records, and decision-making will be easier, with more peace of mind for the family.

Possible costs

Assisted-living costs start at basic services. For a one-bedroom apartment, without assistance, we paid $3,500. If increased care was needed, the care recipient moved to the care side of the assisted-living facility, which may be an extension of the building. The rent there began at $5,000, increasing with any extra services needed. We were paying $5,500 for full care, eventually. This was based on private pay and on Medicare. If your care recipient is on Medicaid, please check if the assisted-living facility accepts it.

Facilities lock down if the flu season or other viruses are rampant. For the flu season, I began getting a flu shot, as I was in the facility daily. Lock down means no one is allowed to enter or leave the facility. During pandemic, residents were quarantined and ate in their rooms. At some of the facilities, if they left the building, re-entry was not allowed.

I'm grateful we did not need to deal with the Covid-19 lockdown with our parents. We knew we would bring our parents to our homes and make adjustments the best we could. Residents were kept in their rooms for more than a year. The mental and emotional distress of lockdowns in a facility was unimaginable.

Foster Care Homes

Usually there are four to six residents with separate bedrooms. Meals are prepared and there is a shared common living space for residents. I interviewed a couple foster care homes locally. They provided no personal service overnight, and I could visit only at specific times during the day. No night visits. It was not a good fit for Mom and me.

Low-Income Housing

It may be located near a Senior Center offering nutritious meals, social outings, pool tables, card games, Bingo, writer's groups, knitting, sewing, stretching, yoga, and medical transport. The housing is often an apartment building, with elevators and private apartments for two people.

Family and friends visited anytime, and hosting small groups in a community area was available with tables, chairs, books, and puzzles. The resident was responsible for ordering medications, cooking, and cleaning. Isolation was a concern if the resident was hesitant to make new friends and join in.

Bus adventure trips were usually offered to the beach, mountains, restaurants, casinos, and special events by the local Senior Center. Another service was free medical equipment of all kinds, available to anyone in need. Meals on Wheels was a program delivering food to the elderly or disabled who were homebound in our area. Check out your local Senior Center. You will be amazed at the services offered. "Seniors" include fifty-five years and older.

Nursing Homes

This was a good fit if the care recipient needed time for rehabilitation. Usually they will be in a shared room with one to three people separated by curtains. All meals are prepared and served. Paid caregivers are often overloaded with residents and did not have time for much personal care, but they did have in-house physical, speech, and occupational therapies offered. The nursing home was a large facility and residents were treated from a more sterile, hospital-type environment, rather than comfy, cozy living. Most residents could stay up to thirty days for rehabilitation due to insurance limits.

Duplexes

This is a fun solution if the care recipient is more independent. A care recipient lives in a one-or two-bedroom apartment with a full kitchen and accessible bathroom. The caregiver lives in the other duplex. Each enjoy their privacy and space. It is great for visitors and family, too.

Duplexes usually have two separate garages connecting them. Unnecessary noise is eliminated, compared to apartment complexes. Landscape or yard maintenance was the resident's responsibility, or both duplexes shared the expense. Maintenance resources may include volunteers, churches, family, friends, Boys/Girls Scouts, or even a meal exchange for some yard work.

Best living style

Enjoy the process of selecting the right living style with the care recipient and yourself. Explore all options available before making a final decision.

Which option fits the best for you?

Which option is best for your care recipient?

What is your second choice and theirs?

What costs will there be in making each of those changes?

Does your care recipient prefer a specific housing choice?

What are the pros and cons of each option?

Here & Now Reflection

MENTAL CLARITY

I painted with acrylics and watercolors. Each one was challenging. It wasn't the paints. It was my lack of experience as a painter. Acrylic paint muddled and watercolor paints ran. Relationships are challenging, especially as a caregiver, and sometimes things look like I paint.

There are medical personnel, administrators, caregivers, errands, bookkeeping, and many more areas to negotiate. Emotions run the gamut in relationships. You have many relationships beyond the care recipient. When I overreacted, trembled in paralyzing fear, or spouted words in anger, creative problem-solving had left the building.

You are learning the art of courageous caregiving. You may need to negotiate through compromises, search for viable solutions, and encourage relationships to thrive. Ask questions. Then, really listen.

You are carefully painting a scene with permanent oils, moveable acrylics and watercolor fluidity. Brush stroke by brush stroke, even sharp edges create beautiful scenes. You are finding your way through relationships. It is worth all the hard work you are putting into it.

Who do you need to have a better working relationship with on your care recipient's behalf? What is the most loving way to do that?

How could you encourage greater mental clarity within challenging relationships?

MOVING EASILY

What would be your mode of moving around your world if your body wouldn't cooperate? A few years ago, my world became very small. Phil and I changed roles for a season. I needed a walker, a commode, medications, and small meals.

When is this severe problem ever going to leave?! My bout lasted about forty-five days.

God talked with me throughout this time of unexpected change. It was shocking and humbling when everything in my world stopped.

What is the mode of moving around for your care recipient? Is their world shrinking?

Walkers

A walker is one of the first pieces of equipment your care recipient may need. If they are less steady on their feet through a stroke or other life event, a walker may be the best choice.

Manual walkers and tennis balls exist together. Most manual walkers are installed with tennis balls to move easily along floors and carpet. Cutting a slit in two tennis balls, wedge them onto the two back legs of the manual walker, not on the wheel area.

Manual walkers come standard, extra-tall, and ones you can lay one or both arms upon and walk upright. If going too fast in a manual walker, use a tall walker, not moving if the person is leaning upon it. It slows the care recipient as the walker stops and no squeezing of a hand brake is needed.

Rolling walkers are an excellent choice if the care recipient is ambulatory. There are rolling walkers with a red laser line in front of them to help guide walking. Rolling walkers require strong hands and the mental capability needed to squeeze the handles for the rolling walker brakes. The height of the walker is important to keep the care recipient upright as much as possible.

Due to several TIAs, Mom rubbed her rolling walker wheels on the edge of walls. It kept her safe from falling down stairs with it, as she hugged the walls and moved along. I nagged her a bit to not rub the walls with her walker, not realizing her spatial cognition was limited. Be patient if your care recipient does likewise at some point along their journey. They are not doing it to irritate you, but usually out of necessity. Extend mercy.

Wheelchairs

Choosing a wheelchair involves many decisions. Wheelchairs need to be measured for width, depth, and back height. Seating clinics are a must for preventing pressure sores and uncomfortable positions. A special cushion will be fitted for the care recipient. Call a hospital rehabilitation unit and they will have resources for seating clinics.

Are footrests needed? Is it important for the care recipient to use their feet as they travel in a wheelchair? They can build leg and core muscles by crossing their ankles and holding their legs up. Care recipients may not be able to move their arms well. Tray and arm-holding devices easily slide onto the arms of a wheelchair. A cup holder may be added to hold beverages.

Check out wheelchair exercises on YouTube to increase your care recipient's strength. Titanium light (t-lite) manual wheelchairs may be used if the care recipient prefers sleek, easy-to-turn-around wheelchairs for tight places. They feature footrests, and require a strong torso, as the titanium wheels are manipulated by hand. Wheelchair gloves are worn to protect the palms.

Manual and travel wheelchairs are the base models for moving abilities when walking is challenging for short or long periods. Travel wheelchairs are excellent for visiting friends, family, or for medical appointments. They are easily folded up and placed in the trunk, but the foot rests must be removed. Large manual chairs are heavy and cumbersome to fold up and load. I purchased the travel chair and it saved my back, and created a quicker pace for Mom and I to get on with living priceless moments, rather than struggling with equipment.

Scooters

Scooters are a quick, easy way for care recipients to go from place to place. Some fold up and fit in trunks easily for transporting. Some are carried on the back of a vehicle with a waterproof cover.

If the care recipient has a stroke or other mental disability, the scooter may be too quick, and difficult to maneuver away from walls, stairs, or other people when they are driving it. Be quick on your toes when a scooter is moving. A woman at an assisted-living facility was a wild card with her scooter, honking the horn for people to dodge out of her way without slowing her scooter down. She came around blind corners like she was on a racetrack.

Power chairs

Power chairs come in front-wheel, mid-wheel, and rear-wheel drive. Care recipients who are unable to use their arms to roll a traditional wheelchair may enjoy a power chair. If they are challenged by spatial issues, a power chair is not a good choice. Cup holders for beverages can be added, as well as custom Roho-type seat cushions to prevent skin issues. You can get a custom-made seat cushion cover in favorite colors; clip a cell phone onto the cup holder, use a custom flat tray fitting on the arm of the chair, or the care recipient may dial their cell phone with a hollow, round plastic stick by blowing into the stick.

If there is a different-ability, there's an accessory made for it. Accessories for power chairs come in all shapes and sizes. Backpacks may hang on the back or side of any type of wheelchair. Power chair custom cushions can hold keys and wallets, making them easy to reach for the care recipient. There are automatic joysticks, goal-post sticks, and knobs for your hand to drive the power chair.

Power chairs can elevate for eye-to-eye conversations, or tilt to a full recline position with the foot pegs raising, too. All extra bells and whistles need to be proven for insurance purposes. If a caregiver has a bad back, then the care recipient is eligible for a power chair that elevates and reclines. Usually, power chairs are eligible to be replaced every five years. However, when a power chair is upgraded, please note insurance doesn't pay for elevating the second time. It will be an out-of-pocket expense. Be kind, but persistent for what your care recipient may need. Listen to your care recipient's perceptions, desires, and needs. Advocate for them, if needed.

Here & Now Reflection

NEVER LOOK BACK

Mom was born the same day as Buzz Aldrin, the Apollo 11 and Gemini 12 astronaut. George Burns was born the same day, a drinking, cigar-smoking comedian. She had many things in common with these two men.

She was adventurous, fearless and loved a good laugh. She never looked back, entertaining no regrets. She always lived in the now, the present moment, often making lemonade from lemons.

Mom was married to my dad for forty-five years. They had a shared career in real estate and made a great life for my brother and I. She was sixty-three years of age when Dad died and went to heaven. Mom was alone.

At sixty-seven years, Mom married her ex-brother-in-law. They were full of adventure; hunting turkeys, ocean fishing, cruising the Caribbean, traveling to many states, and stopping at all the rest stops. God was an active part of their lives, but they were only married three short years. He died and went to heaven. Mom was alone.

At eighty-one years, she married her third husband, a long-time church friend. They laughed, talked, and moved twice during their declining health. They were married five short years. He died and went to heaven. Mom was alone.

Buzz was a famous astronaut who seized the day and never looked back. George Burns laughed, loved his wife, Gracie, and never looked back. Mom, Buzz, and George were full of adventure, never looked back, and never let fear paralyze them.

What are you entertaining from the past and wasting brain cells over?

What do you fear, and when do you need to practice more courage and vulnerability?

What new adventure are you willing to step into?

What is the best choice for your care recipient to move easily from the choices in this chapter?

OPENING DOORS

In the 1980s I had reached the top of my pay scale at a large electronics company.

"Kay Nell, here's your performance review. You can't improve on anything. I see you're at the top of the pay scale as an Executive Secretary, too. I've been thinking it'd be a good opportunity for you to go through the company's management school."

"Wow. You're kidding!"

"No. I think you're ready for it and it'd be a great opportunity for you to advance in the company."

I don't think I'm smart enough to be in management. I don't want to stay at this huge company more than five years. After five years, I'd be fully vested, and then I'll be sucked in and never leave here!

"Thanks for the opportunity, but I think I'm going to pass on the management school training."

At twenty-four years old I slammed the door. I was made for that training and wished I would have walked through the door of opportunity. However, something even better happened: I left the large company and became a successful business owner when opportunity knocked. This time, I ran to the door, and said, "C'mon in!".

Opportunity knocking

Opportunity is knocking. You could ignore the knocking and pretend you don't hear it. You could answer, then when you see the opportunity, you could slam the door in its face.

But what if you welcome the new opportunity?

What if you answer the door with a "Yes!"? Invite it in and visit a bit. You have the opportunity to make a real difference. Will you embrace it, dodge it, or run from it? If you run from it, opportunity will knock again--maybe soon, maybe years from now, maybe tomorrow.

If we run from opportunity, we miss the character growth—the highs, lows, and plateaus. We will grow in character, compassion, wisdom, and love. Some days will be long and arduous. I'm not gonna lie. But the pay-offs are priceless and worth every minute.

Look for opportunities. Do you see other care recipients on your way to your person? It's opportunity knocking.

What is knocking at your door? I dare you to see what's on the other side. Explore ideas with an out-of-the-box perspective. If one idea doesn't work, try another. If the idea falls flat, so what? Allow it to propel you forward to the next opportunity.

Moving forward

Opportunities may be knocking on your door, tickling you with another interesting path. How do you know when to stop caregiving? How do you know when to stop anything? You may know beyond a shadow of a doubt you are ready to stop caregiving. Ask God to give you an answer. Trust your gut, your intuition, your research, and your vision. It doesn't matter if you don't know what you plan to do after you are no longer a caregiver. It's okay. Whatever you choose, check to see if you will regret it in the future—that's always a tell. Then move forward fearlessly.

I applaud you knowing when to leave caregiving. You are a rare breed. Many caregivers keep going until they cannot even move from exhaustion. Good job for knowing what you need and showing the courage to follow through. Good job for making other provisions for your care recipient, if needed. Well done.

Conversations in eyes

What's the mental, physical, and emotional condition of your care recipient? Let's start with their physical needs. Often, care recipients start out needing to be checked in upon. Over time, they may not be able to feed themselves, walk, or make clear decisions.

Mental health ranges from quick and alert to perhaps gradual dementia or Alzheimer's. The care recipient may orient to you only, or to no one at all. Please remember, even if they do not respond verbally, often they will have "windows" where they become lucid. Do not correct them to get things straight. Get into their world. It took me a while to catch on to Mom's new world. Mom often connected through music. One gal offered to play the harp for her.

"Don't let her play the harp. I don't like harp music. I want something peppy."

It was a happy world most of the time, and why not enjoy the conversation with Mom? Even though she was conversing with me only through her eyes for the last few years, she was saying volumes. I understood everything.

Dust devil swirls

What's the purpose of the NASCAR pace car? It leads the other cars around the track. When cars wreck, the pace car comes out and takes the lead again. The pace car offers stability to the other cars. This is what you are offering the people around you in your new caregiving role.

"You should get a job doing this."

"No, thank you. I'm committed to caring for Mom, but I'm a businesswoman at heart, and caregiving is the last job I would make application."

No matter. I heard God call me to it.

Often you fall into caregiving unexpectedly. Camping out under blue skies, birds singing, and instantly an unexpected dust devil swirled through, turning trailers upside down. The dust devil ended as abruptly as it started. That's what happened at the China Hat 100-mile motorcycle race in Bend, Oregon. The aftermath and clean up were still there to be dealt with.

Sometimes it will feel like a dust devil swirled

through your life and turned everything upside down. It may end as abruptly as it started, or it may upend your life for a while. Remember even after all the dust settles, there will still be the aftermath of cleaning up. This is a time to reach out and call for help. It may be a family member, church friend, or a person you least expected to help. If you don't ask, you will never know.

Gentle with yourself

This is a time to be exceptionally gentle with yourself. Work through any anger with a faith pastor, with a counselor, with your God-given wisdom, or with a medical professional. I did not seek professional counseling. It was a gift I could have given myself. If you don't think you have time to seek help, you will find time to bottle up emotions. They will come out at an innocent person, not even related to your circumstances. That was my path during a few moments. My most unfavorite thing to do was apologize when I'd lost my temper. I still apologized, though. You can, too.

This is one of the sharpest times you will be living. Say out loud all the positive things on your heart each day to the care recipient. Now's the time. You don't know how much time you will be with them. Start speaking from your heart now. You may be angry about how things are going. I was. You may be tempted to judge. I did. You may receive judgment from others. I did. Shoo anger and judgment away. You can get down to the business of living and loving well. You're right on time. You're not late. Be gentle with yourself.

Faith practice

If you have a faith practice in place, you have a coping skill many do not. My faith in God is the backbone of my life. Without Him, I would definitely have quit a long time ago, running as fast as I could in the opposite direction. I even would have quit on living a few times in my life. God has made all the difference. A mainstay. A rock. My shelter. He knows every detail of my life. Pray; murmur His words to yourself. Remember how much He wants an intimate walk with you and can hardly wait to meet with you each day. He loves you with all your weaknesses and all your strengths.

You've chosen a good work. It will shape you. It will grow you. It will weary you. It will unnerve you, but it is definitely a good work. And you will have no regrets.

When is anxiety at its peak? Before or after you decide? If you experience the most anxiety before you reach a decision, embrace it. Your challenge is to limit the amount of time it takes to decide. Give yourself a time limit and stick to it.

If you experience anxiety after you make a decision, the lesson will be in teaching yourself confidence in making the best decision and letting it go. Usually, it's the tough decisions in life when we experience the most anxiety. Often there were two "right" answers, and that was where confusion began.

You are smart. You will make good choices. God is guiding you. You may not feel Him or see Him, but He is guiding you. Days may be easy. Days may take every last tool in your toolbox, and you may begin throwing tools.

God is still there, guiding you along the best pathway for your life. Rest easy, my friend. You're right on time.

Here & Now Reflection

MARATHON TRAINING

How do you train for a marathon[8]?

My brother, Jim Boyd, ran several full marathons in Oregon before he was forty-three years of age.

"I can hardly wait to train for my first marathon! It's gonna be awesome. From everything I've read and people I've talked with, I'm training my runs at fifty miles per week. Then, on the weekend, I'll do fifteen to twenty miles of the fifty miles."

At miles twenty-one to twenty-six the pain was brutal. Lactic acid had built up, and Jim's legs (especially his calves) were severely cramping. He limped across the finish line, but his body had taken a beating.

"I can hardly wait to train for my next marathons. I think I'll do one each year, at least. I got an experienced marathon coach, Jim Weber, to train me. He wants me to train at seventy to eighty miles per week. He told me on the steep hills to look down, lengthen my arm swing."

Jim's next marathons, no mile was too tough. Everyone trains: runners, hikers, bicyclists, motorcyclists, and walkers. Training is vital to success.

---

8 https://www.rei.com/learn/expert-advice/training-for-your-first-marathon.html

You are running your own marathon as a caregiver. You never see the finish line at the beginning of the race—you view it during the last mile.

Train yourself and your care recipient in healthy nutrition, hydration, and moving your bodies. This will not happen in a day, but consistently day-by-day training will help you and your care recipient go the distance. Train now as a caregiver, or it will be more than lactic acid building up.

Set your own pace. Although your pace will not be exactly like another caregiver, you will find your pace. Every positive step you take counts—no matter how small.

How can you train yourself for the days ahead?

_____

_____

What do you need to take along?

_____

_____

What pace do you plan to use while caregiving?

_____

_____

Have you ever thought about doing an extended run—3k, 5k, 10k?

_____

_____

Have you ever thought about walking around the block slowly?

_____

_____

How can you improve your nutrition, hydration, and enjoy better health today?

_____

_____

RELIEVING
SUFFERING

Forty-five years ago, we were making a barbed wire fence for cows on our acreage. Phil's parents offered to help us. I never worked on July 4th in my life. It was hot, sweaty, exhausting, and boring.

My mother-in-love looked over at me.

"Let's make some homemade ice cream!"

"Really?"

"Yes! We've been working hard all day. We need to take a break."

"I have no idea how to make homemade ice cream."

"Well, I'll show you how."

A bleak, hard workday—instead of a July 4th carnival. A wonderful memory made, churning ice-cold vanilla ice cream, with my kind mother-in-love. She understood simplicity, reducing life to the basics, and creating something good out of a weary day.

Thirty years later, Phil's elderly parents were living with us. We happily gave them our downstairs bedroom and bathroom, and we were full of hope, as we wanted them comfortable.

My mother-in-love, Leta Pearl, was always content.

She called Kansas home, was from a well-to-do Christian family, and a church pianist. She left it all behind to marry the love of her life, a hard-working cattle farmer. She was a joy for me to be around, required little, and told me family stories. I treasured all my times with her.

Basic essentials

Streamlining your life to the basic essentials to make life easier--hard to apply it in your busy, distracted life in a practical way, and especially as it relates to your care-giving role.

Setting my alarm a bit earlier to unhurriedly arise. Grabbing my brew and sitting in the quiet before the family awakens. I was up at four in the morning listening to birds chirping, because the man I love had been snoring. I got my first cup of java, enjoyed daily quiet time, made breakfast for my tribe, found their lost objects, they found my lost objects, all with a grateful attitude.

If heading to the gym, pack the night before: a towel, clothes/swimsuit, basic make-up, and shoes. Bottomline, you are in charge of your day. You won't be in charge of all the happenings in a day, but you can control your attitude. Streamline your life in ways that work for you. It will make your life easier, and you will experience huge dividends in a short time.

Relieving suffering

I often made things more difficult than needed: cram-ming too much into a day, increasing stress, and rushing everywhere I went. Caregiving can be an intensely stressful time where unexpected situations pop up. I was suffering mentally and emotionally often.

It isn't that you need one person to fulfill all your desires, but you do need someone close that you can talk to honestly. Maybe they sit and listen. Maybe they sit and you both don't talk. There's such a peace in sitting together with a close friend with no need to say a word.

Where are you suffering? Take the time to relieve your suffering as best you can. You would tell someone else to do it. Think of what you need to relieve it. Maybe it's a trip with your family. Maybe it's time alone to think your own thoughts. Discover who you are again. We all need someone close to us to interact with for our own mental health. Maybe it's just taking time for healing tears. Connecting with God and others is everything.

What you see

When you see your care recipient, whom do you see? A person; diminished physically, but their personality is astoundingly wonderful, still? Maybe you saw them suffering, tried to alleviate it, but it was still staring you in the face. It could be their different-ability was glaring at you and you could not move past it; what once was or could have been--gone. See with new eyes. Look. What do you see now?

"Help! Somebody help me! Help! Somebody help me! Help! Somebody help me! Help! Somebody help me!"

I could hear him down the hall from Mom's apartment. The facility's paid caregivers were not coming.

He yelled over and over. His wife had died. His girlfriend with Alzheimer's recently moved to another facility. John had no one. No one came to visit. His own Alzheimer's disease was progressing. He forgot how to get dressed. He forgot why he was here. He forgot why he was walking somewhere. He forgot where his recliner was in the room. The list goes on. John's still yelling for help. I leave my mom's room and walk six doors down, through his open door, into his one-bedroom apartment.

"You're okay, John. I'm here now. What do you need?"

"I don't know what I'm supposed to be doing."

He whined like a lost child. I glanced at a well-worn recliner in the perfect position for the TV that was on.

"You're supposed to be in your recliner. Here, I'll help you."

He is relieved I told him what to do. I placed a cozy blanket on his lap and legs.

"Can you hear the TV, John?"

"Yes. Thank you. I didn't know what to do."

"Okay, John. You're right where you need to be. You're okay."

I turned to leave. An old photo on the maple end table by the door caught my eye: John and his wife. They looked in love, gazing at each other. Sadness enveloped me. Tears brimmed over in my eyes. He is alone and confused. It wasn't supposed to be this way. Where was his family? Did it get too hard for them? It's too hard for John today.

Dementia

You need to keep an open mind and get into your care recipient's world. If dementia is raising its imaginative head, communicate by listening and even agreeing with their thoughts. There is absolutely no point in contradicting their story. It's their story, now. It's reality to them. Embrace it. Welcome it.

If they can no longer talk, remind them of who they were at their best. Repeat their stories back to them.[9] Music speaks when nothing else can and touches the mind, body, and spirit. Try various ways to connect. They are still there, deep down inside. They may not be able to bring the right words up from the file cabinet, but they are there. Heart to heart, you can connect. You make great decisions.

Happiness

You cannot make another person truly happy, but you can make sure they are clean, fed, teeth brushed, and clothes and underclothes clean. You may have done it or you may have asked paid caregivers to do it. Either way, it's your responsibility now--the basic hygiene and cleanliness. If your care recipient is not happy, it's okay. You are responsible for keeping them clean and their basic needs met, not to ensure their happiness all the time.

---

9 https://www.youtube.com/watch?v=hZN1CyEiFNM

Connecting now

If church was an important part of their life before, it will be important now. Often churches will bring communion to those who can no longer attend church.

Read scripture to them. I read Psalm 23 to Mom, and she always began saying it with me. She memorized a lot of scripture in her lifetime, and even though she had dementia, scripture was the glue holding her together still.

Maybe your care recipient sang, played an instrument, or danced. Get creative and make those things happen in some way again. I danced with Mom while she was in bed. I held her hand and bounced around. She thought she was dancing. Connect with who your care recipient was, and create ways to relive those happy memories with them again.

Here & Now Reflection

FORGIVENESS

Forgive yourself; for not doing more, for doing too much, for doing it poorly, for doing it in anger, or for doing it medicated. You are doing your best with what you know and have experienced up to this point in your life.

You're doing enough. You're doing it well. Forgive yourself. Pour a pitcher of grace all over yourself. Relax in it.

Is there something ruminating in your mind about a person you find difficult to forgive?

What would you want God to do with this person, if it was up to you? Unforgiveness destroys the unforgiving person. Forgiveness always frees. Exercise forgiving yourself and others. Free yourself today.

Are you currently suffering today; physically, mentally, emotionally, spiritually? Slow down your thoughts. What way could you move forward rather than sitting in the puddle of your suffering? Do the next thing in front of you. It will often pull you forward. It's too soon to quit. You are worth the time and effort it takes to keep going.

TRUSTING
INSTINCT

I was driving home from a Beth Moore Simulcast at a local church and heard God in my spirit.

"You know, I'll be taking your mom home soon."

Yes. I know.

Although there were four more years of caregiving to go, it gave me peace and helped me prepare for the letting go needed ahead. There was a kindness in the way God talked to my spirit. Such love. He'll speak to you, too. Ask Him what He wants to talk with you about.

Negotiating

Here is where the art of negotiating often takes place. A doctor or nurse may be on staff in a facility and may call the care recipient's doctor directly. In my experience, I found it better to call the doctor myself. When a care recipient is bedfast, sometimes doctors will accept them as patients when they have seen them once. Teleconference or phone calls work for future appointments. This worked extremely well for Mom and I. If you're working with a facility, clarify who will make the call and when to make the call.

Hospice

Maybe you began to work with your local Hospice. Hospice in our county is excellent. Mom was on Hospice five times, and was then moved into Hospice Transition Phase five times. Hospice is usually called if the care recipient has less than one year to live.

Hospice offers a Transition Phase. If the care recipient improved, they entered the Transition Phase of Hospice. In this phase, the Hospice nurse came a little less, but still communicated with doctors and caregivers and made this time more seamless. I talked with them about my mom's health and future health any time day or night. They had eyes on her, so I felt less pressure for a time. A nurse checked in on Mom once or twice per week, advocated with doctors, kept Mom out of needless pain, and helped me sleep easier.

> *"In peace I will lie down and sleep, for you alone,*
> *O Lord, will keep me safe."*
> PSALM 4:8 (NLT)

Seize the day

Decide to make yourself happy by doing something you absolutely love. Please do not wait for permission. Seize the day! We experience guilt for taking time off when we have our own health and time to care-give, but this is no time for guilt. Usually, guilt is about using the words "should have." "Should" never changed anything. This is time for you to recharge, renew, and rejuvenate.

I felt overwhelmed and completely exhausted.

My adult son, Jordan, always asks me the right questions.

"Mom, will you come back better than you are now?"

"Uhhh...YES!"

"Then go, Mom."

My oasis was less than an hour away from my home. I checked into a beautiful suite. Ordered room service. Dined vegan at the in-hotel restaurant. I was not vegan, but it was fun to try it on for size. Slept. Read my bible. Watched TV. Journaled. Listened to podcasts. And you know what? I reconnected with me. My likes, my dislikes. My incredible sense of humor, even when I'm alone. I had truly lost myself in caregiving. I gave myself permission to seize the day.

"My heart has heard you say, "Come and talk with me."
And my heart responds, "Lord, I am coming."
PSALM 27:8 (NLT)

Mixing days

"I can't believe they're going away on vacation while their mother is in rehab for four weeks!"

You know who made those comments? Someone never in the throes of caregiving. They didn't know the emotional toll it took or the vast aloneness a caregiver experiences daily.

The timing seemed completely off. Eight days into my early retirement, ready to enjoy adventures with my five-year-old son, Jordan, it wasn't fair. I didn't remember applying for a caregiver position, and it was the last job I ever wanted. I was an entrepreneur, a forty-something businesswoman who made things happen. I felt best with young people, leading, organizing, and working in my strengths.

Now my happiest days were mixed with my saddest days. This was a new experience. I perceived the timing was off, but it didn't matter.

Caregiving kicked down the door and said, "I'm heeeeere!"

Who are you?! I didn't invite you in, but you're lounging on my couch and it seems you're here to stay.

The following years reshaped me; bent me, twisted me, flattened me. I didn't sign up for it, didn't want to do it, and didn't know what I was doing. It was a club no one wanted to be in. Caregiving was a trial-by-fire experience. I was forced to trust my decisions, trust my ability, trust my strength, trust my reliability, and trust my God every single day. It changed my life for the better, forever.

Opportunity windows

Nina was a middle-aged woman with dark hair, and kindness overflowing. She was a paid caregiver for Mom at her assisted-living facility. Nina rushed to me as I came through the double doors for my daily visit with Mom.

"You won't believe what your mom said to me today. It freaked me out!"

"Oh, no, I'm sorry, what did she say to you?"

"No, I was shocked! She was speaking Truth. I was feeding her lunch and with complete clarity, she said,

'You and me. We're not long for this world, but it's okay. We'll be in heaven together, soon." Then your mom went back to not talking."

Nina had received a recurring cancer diagnosis. She believed Mom was an angel talking to her and encouraging her. A few days later, Nina brought Mom a little angel to sit on the piano in her room. And now, decades have passed and the angel sits in Mom's china cabinet in the corner of my dining room. Nina quit work and I lost track of her, but I know she carried the vision God gave her through Mom.

You will learn to trust, too. Even when trusting God, I did caregiving the right way, the wrong way, the yelling way, the angry way, the peaceful way, the graceful way, and the loving way. Allow caregiving to change you. It will build your character, but it may not look pretty some days.

Trust your instincts

As a teenager, if I knew Mom was coming home at a certain time, I'd wait until the last possible moment to do the chores she asked of me. They would be done when she walked through the door. She didn't know I watched TV, listened to music at high decibels, and spent hours talking on the phone

The key to ensuring safety for your care recipient is to be alert, and visit at various times of the day or night, if the care recipient is in a facility. I didn't let the paid caregivers know when I'd be visiting when she was in an assisted-living facility for a season.

Your care recipient's wellbeing is what counts at any time. In my over 65,000 hours of unpaid caregiving, swing shift (10:00 pm-6:00 am) was when care significantly declined. Usually, no managers were present, no meals were served, and no residents were out and about. The day shift was more active; supervisors were in abundance and the facility was humming like a well-oiled machine. Many times, it depended on the caregiver assigned to your care recipient on any given day, as to level of care. You will know the ones who are exceptional and the ones to beware. Trust your instincts.

One of the most luxurious assisted-living facilities had the most negligent administrator. The not-as-glamorous assisted-living facility had a pro-active administrator, and was easier to negotiate. The integrity of the facility is critical. If they are negligent, file a written report at the local Department of Aging and also file one with the local Ombudsman. The Ombudsman number is posted in each facility. If you have access to a journalist, use the resource. You are a caregiver for your care recipient, but you also want to prevent negligence for any other care recipient in the future.

Trust your timing. Trust your ability. Trust your instincts. Trust your God.

Here & Now Reflection

HOLINESS

Holiness was there in front of me. A spiritual path I could take. A path many others missed. I know a few of the ones who missed it.

Some of Mom's Christian friends were confused.

"I've been praying for your mom to die. I mean, what good is she now? I just hate she doesn't know anyone. I don't know how you do it. I could never do it."

The comment stemmed from frustration they could not reconcile in their spiritual life anyone suffering. They couldn't look at Mom when she could no longer move about, think clearly, and help others.

They missed the holiness found there in her room. I didn't judge them. The same lesson will appear again for them to choose. They lost their way. They took another path, and refused to take the long path Mom was on. They were afraid. Fear overtook them and paralyzed them. They looked away and hoped her declining health wasn't catching.

The last part of their comment, they were thinking that if their loved one was experiencing the same thing, they couldn't possibly be there for them. They failed to remember God provided the strength, not ahead of time, but in each moment.

He didn't give me strength for thirteen years of caregiving ahead of time, but He gave me strength every single moment of every single day. Sometimes I forgot He was there with me. He was still there, waiting for me to glance His way. And when I did, there He was, giving me all I needed for the moment.

I commend you, right now, for choosing to take the path, and allowing yourself to ride this roller coaster and spiritual journey. May you find hope, strength, and encouraging words to urge you on in the holiness of caregiving. You can do it with tenacity and gentleness. Most of all, may you find Him there—going before you, walking beside you.

What does your spiritual path look like in the last year?

Are you having conversations with God all along the way of caregiving?

Do you see His holiness in your days?

What could you offer another caregiver in the way of encouragement?

MISSING PIECE

In the 1960s my brother, Jim, and I had the chore of walking around the corner to a dairy farm each week to bring home fresh milk in two glass gallon jugs. Clara was also a local grade school teacher and she shared the dairy farming with her husband, Bill. They went to the same church before Jim and I were a twinkle in our parents' eyes.

"I want you kids to go get two glass gallons of milk from Clara & Bill's dairy. Jim, you're in charge."

"Okay, Mom."

"Let's go, Kay Nell."

Jim was eleven, and I was six.

"Look what I can do, Kay Nell! I can swing the jug in a full circle up and back down! Watch me!"

Jim easily swung the milk jug up high above his ahead and brought it back down in a circular motion.

"Jim, I think I can do it, too!" My missing piece.

I mimicked him. The glass milk jug went high up, as my little feet lifted me and crashed me down on the ground.

My right palm landed in the glass shards. A deep

gash between my thumb and index finger rushed us to our neighborhood doctor's home. I learned about antiseptic, numbing agents, stitches, and a cast for several weeks. My right hand still shows the scar, but I practiced piano and I could reach farther than an octave in the years ahead.

Memories fading

Clara and I crossed paths again at my mom's assisted-living facility in the winter of both their lives.

"Clara, you could stop by and visit Mom in her apartment anytime. I know she'd love seeing you."

"No. I don't think I will. I prefer to remember her as she used to be...fun, active; a leader, helper, and businesswoman." She didn't want to see any suffering. Clara's missing piece.

Clara went to her heaven several years earlier than Mom. When I think of Clara, I touch my scar, and think of the fun I had trying to do anything Jim could do.

Are there significant spaces missing in your care recipient's immediate memory? Are they asking the same questions over and over? Do they forget who you are?

Mom had vascular dementia and it was creeping slowly. She began forgetting how to get home when she was at a grocery store. She had a couple fender benders. She placed items in drawers that were completely in the wrong place.

Medication sometimes postponed the onset of memory issues. There were new studies being done all the time. There were several medications doctors recommended. Not every medication works in every case. Seek medical advice. Contact a teaching university, a naturopath, watch podcasts, or do your own research. Check out Elon Musk's groundbreaking research in his Neuralink[10] company. If your care recipient's memory is fading a bit, do the steps to alleviate the symptoms as much as possible.

Mastering self-discipline

Art was over six feet tall, and in his younger years he served in the Army. As a ninety-year-old resident, he led a hard, boot camp-style exercise class three times a week in his assisted-living facility. He was a journalist, but nearly blind now, and he started writing for the local newspaper, using mega-sized fonts on his computer. His mind was sharp.

Playing the piano without sheet music quite a few people can do. But Art's music was melancholy, full of passion, always classical and brimming with emotion. He didn't enjoy playing for people, so I sneaked in, sat far behind him as his fingers glided across the baby-grand piano and fed my soul. I finally had the courage to ask him.

"Art, how do you play so well?"

"Oh, I don't read music or memorize songs. I make them up as I go."

His piano playing stopped people in their tracks. They sat and listened out of his view. Art was elderly,

---

10   https://www.youtube.com/watch?v=iOWFXqT5MZ4

suffered with severe macular degeneration, and felt loneliness after his wife passed. Art's missing pieces.

However, each day he awoke early, led callisthenic exercise classes, created melodic, passionate piano music on the spot, and kept moving forward. Art mastered self-discipline. Surely, I can, too. So can you. Art was brave and didn't know it. You may not know it, but you're mastering self-discipline and brave, too.

Love and forgive

I did my best. Thirty-six years of birthdays, weekends, sleepovers, shopping trips, campouts, vacations, and celebrations, were not enough. One day she was loving me and the next day unforgiveness was crawling under her door and darkening her heart.

I did my best. She has not spoken to me, nor told me why she wears unforgiveness like a suit of armor, against me and others, for over decades. She sits alone by the cold fire of unforgiveness. She has endured unimaginable losses in the past few years. A missing piece. My prayer for her is:

"Dear friend, I pray that you may prosper in every way and be in good health physically just as you are spiritually."
3 JOHN 2 (CSB)

Family life helps us learn how to love, forgive, and move forward. It's a choice, though. In my view, life is too short to be wasted in anger and unforgiveness. There is no time for regrets. Forgive; even if the other person never asks you for forgiveness. Forgive anyway. Phil,

Jordan, Nicole, and I allow ourselves space to forgive, if needed, and move forward. We make every effort to love, above all. We do our best. Life is short. As far as it depends upon you, make sure there's no missing pieces.

I held Jordan's hand when he was small; jumped in mud puddles, laughed at silly jokes, fed sugar cubes to the neighbor's horse, and said hello to the neighbor's dog, Barney.

Later as a teenager, Jordan was talking to our neighbor.
"Hey, how's Barney?"
"Who's Barney?"
"Oh, you know, your little beagle dog."
"Oh, you mean Scud."
"What?!"
"His name is Scud." Jordan couldn't wait to get home.
"Mom, you told me the dog's name was Barney! His name is Scud!"
"I guess I named him Barney from the TV show, and I started believing it myself.

I'm so sorry. That must have been embarrassing for you. Will you forgive me?"
"Sure. It was kind of funny. It makes more sense his name is Scud."

Family loves, forgives, and moves forward. No missing pieces.

Desire to share

God's given you the desire to share all He has gifted you with and it's meant to be shared with others. Playing Clair de Lune, Adagio, or Largo on the piano has brought me to tears; not because the notes were played perfectly. The joy was in the practice, and it was glorious. Maybe you play the piano much better than me; like my niece, Heidi, by the time she was in elementary school. Use it. Enjoy it. Share it. Pure joy awaits with no missing pieces.

Here & Now Reflection

EYES OF THE HEART

Music feeds the soul. When nothing else is working, play some music. Music soothes. Music calms, settles, and uplifts, whether suffering with dementia, spinal-cord injury, nerve pain, or severe anxiety.

Music and singing touch people by quieting their minds, letting their minds relax. Music doesn't need to be slow and heavy. Uplifting music with a fun, quick beat may speak better. Mom never drank, but on her ninetieth birthday, dementia living with us daily, she wanted to sing "There Is A Tavern in The Town" over and over, with her family all around her. Playing her request on the piano, we were laughing and singing our hearts out. She smiled broadly, moved her feet in the bed and sang softly along. Music speaks to the soul. Her singing soothed our souls. A family's sacred moment. Embrace those moments with your care recipient.

If you can get past yourself, you begin to see your caregiving and advocacy tasks with the eyes of your heart. There came a time I noticed there were people God was putting in my direct path. While my one-track mind focused on visiting Mom, God spoke to my heart and showed me all the daily miracles around me in the assisted-living facility. Look up. You will see them. You will realize you're not only there for your care recipient, but for others as well. If you dare to look, your life will become richer and you will see daily miracles in the most unlikely places.

Whether your loved one knows you today or doesn't, you can touch them. They know your love by the kindness and warmth of your touch. Words are not required. Response is not required. You are the hands of God, showing compassion, kindness, gentleness, and love today.

You may even get a response that indicates your loved one doesn't choose to be touched right now. Not all is lost. Sit or walk with them in silence, if needed. Wouldn't you love to not need to speak in moments, but bask in the presence of your beloved person sitting with you? Requiring nothing from you; expecting nothing in return, but your presence. You're not wasting your time. In fact, you are doing a great work caregiving. No one may see, except God. It's enough.

Who is in your path daily, but you do not acknowledge them?

Who could you free from your relentless expectations?

Where are your missing pieces?

TRAVELING HOME

My day started like any other; devotions, moving my body, garden club, and visit Mom. The phone rang.

"Kay Nell?"

"Yes."

"This is Linda from your mom's room. She fell out of bed, on her face. The lady who lives on the first floor below your mom's apartment heard a loud noise and called us. We rushed to your mom's place and found her on the floor by the left side of her bed. She doesn't seem to be responding well, but nothing appears broken or damaged."

"Okay. I'll be right there."

It was an eight-minute trip to Mom's after moving to the edge of town. Before moving from our country home by a creek, we were twenty-five long minutes away.

"Mom? Mom?"

She looked at me with those deep brown eyes; beginning at the edge of her lips and coming across slowly, a small grin formed.

There she is.

My breath and shoulders dropped away from my ears.

"Mom, would you like a little water?"

She turned her head away.

"Mom, would you like a little applesauce?"

Again, she turned away. I knew her. It was her definite no.

The rest of the day was a blur; I offered food, juices, water, changed diapers, and sat in a chair comfortably holding her hand. After I called Hospice, the nurse came and confirmed what I already knew in my gut. It would be a matter of twelve to forty-eight hours. Nothing pried me away from her, even into the wee hours of the morning; I was unable to resist leaving her.

She was on the journey home and I didn't want to miss a second. Rattling permeated her labored breathing now. She previously taught me with friends we saw passing heavenward, sometimes a death rattle happens before the last breath.

It was getting close.

At five in the morning, the death rattle suddenly stopped. It was the longest night of my life hearing the rattled breathing. When it stopped, her room was silent, and I opened my eyes. A dark, evil foreboding overtook her room. Satan was lingering. After all, death was his thing. He still hoped to steal, slaughter, and destroy her last moments. She faithfully, actively, lived for God from eighteen to ninety-six years of age, taught Jim, me, and hundreds of others all about her Jesus. Church was our second home and all our families were believers.

Spirit knows spirit

I rose up from the recliner and what happened next can only be explained in the spiritual realm. It wasn't me, it was Jesus. Yes, I was the one talking, but it flowed like a mighty river out of my mouth; like a fire that could not be stopped. Instantaneously, I was praying in the Spirit loudly, commanding in Jesus' Name the evil one, "Out! You cannot touch her in Jesus' Name."

Within a half hour, the entire atmosphere in Mom's room changed immediately. God's peace and His presence were thick, palpable once again and remained.

She was quiet, at peace, no bruises or pain, but definitely on the path home, and I was humbly grateful I was with her. The day wore on and I saw the differences in her from the previous thirteen years. Her breathing was shallower, but she could still hear me. Reading Psalm 23 and singing quietly "How Great Thou Art" fed my spirit, and hers as well. They were her favorites. Checking her feet and legs, I could see the discoloring of her earthly body, the one I knew and loved. It was shutting down, and her spirit was getting ready for the journey home.

Family arrives

Time to call my extended family: Phil; my brother, Jim; his wife, Cheryl; my nieces, Heather and Heidi. A nephew, Jesse, came to see his Grandma. He had a heart for her. They had a thing between them and he always kissed her cheek and said, "The Kissing Bandit will be back soon!" before he left her.

Today, he knew it was the last time in her presence. We respectfully filed out of Mom's room so he could finish well with her.

We heard him say it.

"One last kiss from the Kissing Bandit."

He slowly walked out of her apartment, tears flowing; we all hugged and he steadily sauntered down the hall, processing his grief.

My friend for fifty years, Cindy, came to sing some of Mom's favorite hymns by her bedside. The family was grateful; although our family was musical, she did what none of us could emotionally do—sing.

The family took turns sitting by Mom's bedside, finished up the things we'd said thousands of times to her: how much we loved her, revisited fun memories with her, and softly spoke love into her ears. Breathing was getting less and less. She gently stopped breathing. The second her spirit left her body, we all knew she'd completed her journey home to heaven, and she was basking in His glorious presence.

The body who gave birth to me at forty-one years of age, nursed me, rocked me to calm ear aches, learned to ride a bike at fifty years of age so we could ride together, unconditionally loved me through my sassy teen years, cleaned and helped move us into many homes, and always ready to go anywhere, without asking where we were going. I knew she was Home. And I also realized all of us were heading towards Home, too.

Mom's often quoted verse and message follows:

*"…the time for my departure is close. I have fought the good
fight, I have finished the race, I have kept the faith. There is
reserved for me in the future the crown of righteousness, which the
Lord, the righteous Judge, will give me on that day, and not only
to me, but to all those who have loved His appearing."*
2 TIMOTHY 4:6-9 (CSB)

"Dying will be like dropping my coat and I will be
in Jesus' presence. When I die, do not think of me as
dead, for I will be more alive than I have ever been! I
was born in the flesh in 1914 and born in the Spirit in
1932. My flesh will die, but my Spirit immediately lives
on forever with Christ. And I'm waiting to see you all
again! See you there!"

The family was crying when I turned towards Phil.
Our eyes met, and we knew we had no regrets; a job
well-done. We high-fived each other with tears in our
eyes and fell into each other's arms. His parents had lived
down the hall from my mom's apartment for a few years.
Phil's dad, Boyd, journeyed home six years prior, and
his mom, Leta, four years prior. We were both unable to
resist caregiving for our parents and their spouses during
their declining health. Leta was the cream of the crop,
contented, a hard-worker, and family-oriented fun. Boyd
was a hard worker, provided for his family, but his health
decline was a tough, lingering one.

Still learning

The paid caregivers arrived in my mom's room when I
told them she had died.

"Would you like to help us give her a bed bath?"

The young woman was talking to me.

"What? Why would you do that? I don't understand. She's gone."

"We do it to show respect and dignity for your mom."

"Great. Yes. I'll help. Show me what to do."

Family sauntered into the hallway, grieving. Washcloths, towels, and baby wipes were all we needed. Eventually, we gently rolled Mom to her right side.

The silent, holy reverence the caregivers and I shared was priceless, and I knew, once again, I was unable to resist even now.

Here & Now Reflection

SUFFERING

Darling, I'm here for you.

Darling, I know you are there.

Darling, I know you suffer; that is why I'm here for you.

Darling, I suffer. I'm trying my best to practice. Please help me.[11]

Do others know you are there for them, no matter what?

What is your plan if your care recipient passes while you are their caregiver? Do you want to be there? Why or why not?

Do you see someone you love suffering in some way? How can you reach out to them?

---

11 https://www.youtube.com/watch?v=UEUxFNkISnU

Do you let your loved ones know you are suffering some days?

_____

_____

MEMORIES FROM
THE HEART

My mom, Kathryn Boyd, shared memories written on her heart through the years. May you laugh, remember, and write memories on the hearts of those you love.

My very first memory was the birth of my sister, Louise. I was five-years-old. My mother was 28-years-old and my father was 33-years-old when I was born in 1914.

We lived in a sod house in Bridgeport, Nebraska. Our home was covered on the outside with cement and on the inside with plaster. There were two bedrooms downstairs, kitchen, living room, and one large room upstairs. This housed my parents, my 5 brothers, 4 sisters, and I.

My nicknames were M.K., Shorty, Katie, Kats and Punk. My name was originally Martha Catherine, but I changed it during school to Kathryn and never used my first name.

My favorite movie was Nelson Eddy and Jeanette McDonald in *Dream Boat*. My favorite actress was Clara Bow, known as the "It" girl.

I loved my dad because he was fun. My Mom was honest and calm. At 8 years of age, I won second prize in a foot race and got a silk handkerchief.

Our family cars were a 1918 Model T with celluloid curtains, 1932 Chevy, 1936 Ford, 1951 Buick, 1956 Oldsmobile. I got my license when I was 16-years-old without any kind of a test.

First time I caught a fish was in 1983 on Don's son, Robert's boat. Since Don was my brother-in-law, then my second husband, Robert was also my nephew. He always called me "Auntie Mom." First time I gambled was in 1981 at Lake Tahoe with Don.

My loves: Dale Dally—I was 14 and he was 18. True puppy love. I had to take my sister, Cornelia, along on our date. Jimmy Jimmerson; my children always laughed at that name.

I've been married three times, and each one died. Ellis Boyd (1932-1977), Don Rieck (1981-1984) and Harry Gibbs (1996-2001).

Most memorable person I ever met in Forest Grove, Oregon was Ella Hutchins. I enjoy small towns, home cooking, restaurants, early rising, doing my own hair, spending money, living in a house, and one husband at a time.

As a child, I never enjoyed making my bed, picking up my clothes, wiping the dishes, taking a nap or staying in on a rainy day.

I love to get up in the early morning, talk to strangers, work with flowers, cook special dishes, clean house, and move to a new home. I hate buying a new car.

For my high school senior year, my Aunt Louise bought me a red chiffon and velvet dress. For my Junior/Senior banquet, my Grandpa Hume bought me a long, blue formal.

My first train rides were in 1926 to Casper, Wyoming and in 1928 to Denver, Colorado.

Some places I traveled to: Australia, New Zealand, Fiji, Samoa, Hawaii, Jamaica, Puerto Rico, Jerusalem, Vancouver BC, China, Hong Kong, Mexico, Greece, Italy, Egypt, Jordan, and all over Europe and the United States. Fiji was my favorite place.

The funniest joke I ever played on someone was on April 1, 1936—vinegar as juice on canned cherries and salt in the sugar bowl.

Scariest thing I ever did was in Bridgeport, Nebraska, I

stepped into a ten-foot hole in the Belmont Ditch and nearly drowned. I was leery of water ever since.

I lived on a farm growing up and milking cows. My most embarrassing moment was in the 10th grade and I could not think of the word "udder" for a teacher question, so I said "Cow's breast". Everyone roared!

I always wanted to be a Nurse.

The weirdest thing happened in Nebraska. We had a prairie fire. School was cancelled so we could fight fire all afternoon.

The funniest thing happened growing up. My sister, Helen, fell in the outside toilet when she was about four-years-old!

My favorite sayings were:

Many hands make short work.

As through life you go, five things observe with care—to whom you speak, of whom you speak, and how, and when, and where.

If at first you don't succeed, try, try again.

My parents said when I started to speak as a young girl, I spoke early and all the time. Later on I was timid, shy, romantic, lean, and later on, adventurous. At thirteen I first wore lipstick and washed it off before I went home from school. At fourteen, I had my first date. At fifteen I had my first cigarette. At sixteen, I had my first drink.

My favorite hobbies now are calling on the sick, embroidery and crocheting.

My first paycheck was from Kepler's grocery store in 1931; Bridgeport, Nebraska. I worked 12 hours/day, 6 days/week and made $9.00/week. This is where I met my first husband, Ellis. We took our honeymoon in a Model T at 25 miles per hour from Bridgeport, Nebraska, to live in Oregon, where his parents lived. The first rent we paid in Oregon was $50/year in 1932 on eight acres in Dilley. Later In Hillsboro, we paid $6/ month for an apartment.

My two birthday surprise parties were given by my sister-in-law and later on, by Kay Nell. My favorite colors are blue and red. My favorite flowers are gladiolas & tulips. My favorite perfume is White Shoulders and Aromatic Elixir by Clinique.

My favorite day of the year is Christmas. My favorite time of the day is morning. My favorite musical instruments are the violin, piano, saxophone, and drums. My favorite songs are *How Great Thou Art, Just a Closer Walk with Thee, Why Me, One Day at a Time, and Alone with God.* My favorite Bible scriptures are Psalm 23, Philippians 3:13 and Philippians 4:4-9.

PRACTICAL TIPS INDEX

— Practical Tip —
Bathing

Daily bathing is preferred. If non-ambulatory, a roll-in/walk-in shower or tub is good. Place a towel on the seat to prevent slipping as the care recipient sits. A roll-in shower is possible with a hoyer, placing the care recipient in a shower chair. Shower chairs are usually made of PVC pipe, with a netted seat and back. They are available in waterproof wheelchairs with a soft seat, and a hole in the seat for hard-to-reach areas.

What best suits your care recipient? If your care recipient is non-ambulatory, some kind of a bath may be every other day. Keep the care recipient clean between bathing using a baby-wipe product. Look for baby wipes for sensitive skin, non-allergenic, and unscented.

Towels are essential to the care recipient's health. Select ones requiring only one pass of the towel to dry off. Quality towels are usually sufficient. Order on-line from hospitality sites. Norwex[12] towels are thirsty towels and on-line, but they do require separate washing.

Bath towels, washcloths and hand towels are not all the same. Hotel-quality towels are often the least expensive and the best. Find the softest, most absorbent, and time-saving towels for you and your care recipient. Bathing is vital to your care recipient's well-being.

---

12 Norwex.com

—— Practical Tip ——
Bed & quilted underpad positioning

Equipment needed:
Reusable quilted underpad 34" x 36"
(100% machine washable and odor controlling)

This is for care recipients who are in bed most of the day or non-ambulatory. After several months of Mom in her bedroom, the walls began closing in on us with no view, low lighting, and confined space.

I moved her electric bed into the living room--featuring big windows, more space, more light, more seating for visitors, and my piano close by--was perfect. Her grandchildren placed encouraging posters on her ceiling so she had something to look at other than the stark white. Think outside the box. If there's a bedroom, the bed doesn't necessarily need to be in that room. Use the bedroom for storage, place an extra TV, and comfy chairs. Visitors could step away and have a few moments to themselves.

Changing a quilted underpad is easy. Roll the care recipient gently towards you, with your palms on their back and legs. Roll the soiled underpad up to the care recipient's back. Lay the new rolled up underpad on the bed up to the care recipient's back. Release them onto their back gently.

Go to the opposite side of the bed and gently roll the care recipient towards you. Remove the soiled, rolled up quilted underpad. Spread out the last half of the new underpad and roll the care receiver onto their back. Prevent bedsores by making the underpad totally smooth under your care recipient. Never pull the underpad from under the care recipient without rolling them, as it may easily tear their skin.

Always explain to the care recipient what you plan to do before and while you're doing it. Even if the care recipient has dementia, it's a matter of respect. Most of their lives are out of control at this point. Speaking kindly to your care recipient shows value, respect, and love. And isn't it what we all want: to experience great love in day-to-day living?

—— Practical Tip ——
Bibs

A necessity if your care recipient is non-ambulatory and unable to eat at a table. Mom eventually could not feed herself.

My sister-in-love, Cheryl, made several terrycloth bibs, covering Mom from her neck to her lap. The neck was Velcro and super easy to put on. Cheryl used easy-to-launder terrycloth and bound the edges with seam-binding tape. They looked like new after washing.

Ask the seamstress in the care recipient's friends or family to make these bibs. They may enjoy making bibs, but are not comfortable feeding your care recipient. It's all about teamwork, resources, and creative problem-solving.

— Practical Tip —
Cardio

Cardio revives you. It clears the mind and releases endorphins. Getting the heart rate up and sweating a bit helps you solve challenges easier, and sleep is sweeter. Yoga is a great release and involves breaking a sweat and stretching your body in ways you normally wouldn't.

Keep the balance of people vs. alone time agreeing with your personality. This may not be easy for you. Positive, uplifting, encouraging people will help you be more at ease, unlike those who could care less about your caregiver role and only talk about their own problems. They don't call them "challenges," but problems. They talk in circles. Forever talking about the problem. Never wanting a resolution, but only to maintain the status quo. This is no time for you to bring those conversations up close to you.

It is a time to uplift, move your body, and encourage others. You are inspired. You may fear something, but you push past it and move forward. Embrace your favorite cardio activity, the one you take pleasure in, moving your body.

— Practical Tip —
Care recipient information

Gather the following information onto one document. It will save you hours of time filling our repetitive forms. When given a form for your care recipient, give them a copy of your document and hand it all back to them. They were always grateful.

Name
Address
Contact phone
Emergency name and phone
Date of birth
Social security number
Medicare number, secondary insurance number & phones
Supplemental drug plan number/company & phone
Medical History
Surgeries, dates, and results
Family Medical History
Parents (Alive? Deceased?) age, health challenges
Siblings (Alive? Deceased?) age, health challenges
Medications
Prescriptions, time taken and dosage of each
Vitamins, dosage of each
Aspirin, Advil
Physicians: list all doctors the care recipient is a patient, including phone, address, and specialty
Diagnosis/Symptoms

If there is a significant complaint, keep a history of the date and how it resolved each time (i.e., bladder infections, spasms, insulin, etc.) This saves time in the future and helps you know how to resolve repetitive health challenges.

CARE RECIPIENT LOG

As a caregiver, keep a care recipient log for the family. It helps to keep everyone up-to-date on any adjustments or changes needed. The log needs to include columns for the date, time, the care given, and the caregiver's initials.

—— Practical Tip ——
Care recipient manicures by caregiver

Equipment:
Gentle nail file
Nail clippers
Nail cuticle clipper
Cuticle orange stick
Fingernail base coat and top coat (fast dry, if possible)
Quick dry spray
Washcloth
Small towel
Optional: Two people can each manicure a hand and save time, if you have a willing friend like I did.

Fill a small bowl half-full of water and a drop or two of gentle hand soap. Place a small towel under their hand. Soak their nails for about five to ten minutes. The longer you soak, the easier the manicure will be for you. Mom was in her electric lift recliner or in bed when I was giving her a manicure, and I held the bowl to avoid spillage.

After soaking, toss the water/soap solution out. Dry the hand with a small towel. Gently push the cuticles back with the orange stick. Use the nail cuticle clipper to carefully snip away dead skin around the cuticles.

Clip nails and file to the desired shape. Do not clip the nails too close in the corners, as it may cause in-grown nails and inflammation. If this happens, a solution of Epsom salt soak may help. You will need to use your own discretion here. Call a physician if it is a stubborn inflammation.

Take a washcloth and wipe the nails dry. Paint on the base coat. Let dry. You may need to hold your care recipient's hand until their nails are dry. Paint the top coat on. This could be a color, if your care recipient would enjoy it. Dry top coat. There are quick dry nail colors, shellac, and quick dry sprays. Use the one easiest for you and your care recipient.

Manicurists are often in assisted-living facilities for residents, but if the resident cannot come to the manicure station, these directions will assure their nails receive good care. It is compassionate, respectful, and honoring to allow your care recipient to help participate in their life and care as much as possible.

You are daring to learn new ways. Good job!

— Practical Tip —

Care recipient massage by caregiver

Equipment:
Massage oil (grapeseed oil, coconut oil, or olive oil)
Heated flax neck pillow (u-shaped)

Create a relaxing atmosphere with gentle music or low lighting. Heat the flax neck pillow in the microwave for thirty seconds at a time until it is warm, but not hot. Test it on your skin. Place it around their neck. Massage in long strokes with light pressure. If your care recipient is unable to turn onto their stomach, you can still massage all areas. Start with the legs and move completely around the leg, finishing with a great foot massage. Some days, Mom lifted her leg up upon request, helping access the underside of her leg. After the legs and feet, continue to the arms.

Mom could not move her left arm eventually, so I lifted her arm as I massaged. It's also a good time to check on underarm care. She tended to sweat under the arm that she couldn't move. If her paid caregivers did not bathe well, sores developed. Her underarm sores healed well by cleaning gently under her arm with a washcloth and warm water, drying it thoroughly, and applying Aquaphor liberally. A few days of doing this and it completely cleared up. If it doesn't clear up quickly, consult the care recipient's physician.

After massaging legs, feet and arms, I massage her neck and face. I stood at the head of Mom's bed, leaning over to massage her face, forehead, chin, and neck. The chin and neck were easy to massage from this position. I pulled up gently on each side of her face and she often lifted her neck to allow easy access. It showed how much she was enjoying her massage.

Mom never received a massage in her earlier years. She thought pedicures, manicures, and massages were a decadent waste, and she found value helping elderly people. In later years, she loved massages, manicures, and pedicures. For a while, I paid a masseuse to come to her apartment, but eventually schedules changed, and I became her masseuse.

The purpose of a caregiving massage is primarily to touch, pamper, and stimulate circulation, but you may find a massage is therapeutic and calming for you, as well. As I was giving her a massage, I was also taking care of myself by experiencing the peaceful flow of it.

God intends us to find joy moments in the caregiving life. He desires good for you, for every detail of your life. Look for those moments. Watch for Him. He's right there with you and your care recipient. He is omniscient (all-knowing), omnipresent (everywhere at the same time) and omnipotent (all-powerful). He knows what you are experiencing, He is constantly there with you, and He can do anything; everything is possible.

— Practical Tip —
Care recipient papers

In a spiral notebook, make a list of medications, primary care physicians and specialist physicians with phone numbers, plus a family health history (living and deceased). Place it in their room, somewhere near the phone or on a counter. Add your Healthcare Representative and Power of Attorney forms. Add numbers to call in the event of death, and in the order you prefer.

Carry one copy with you at all times and one in your car. Get the advance directive form as soon as possible, before you are in an emergency room somewhere, trying to get signatures. Not pretty. You can get them online or from an office supply store. You may need to read and explain each question so they can choose their answers, if they are not already in the late stages of dementia.

Mom did her advance directive when she was completely lucid, years before her first stroke. I cannot stress to you how much relief I felt in looking at the advance directive years later, when complications were an everyday occurrence. The advance directive was my saving grace. When my brain was mashed potatoes, and Mom's memory was floating off through the air like a dandelion puff, reading it reassured me I was making decisions based on what she truly wanted. It was one way of honoring her when things were as clear as mud.

One caveat though: if surgery is needed, and they are not cognizant, the stress level may soar. There was a surgical form. The surgical form forced the decision she be kept alive heroically during surgery, or no heroics if her body stats dropped.

She was in her late eighties then, and dementia moments were coming more often. A tough call. It was called the "hot pink form" by hospital staff. Try to make the decision now, rather than when they are being rolled into emergency surgery. On a personal note, we decided on heroics, if necessary, but no ventilator or tubes connected to her post-surgery. The medical team was satisfied. We sat on pins and needles, hoping our decision didn't have to be applied. The outcome was good.

Later on, Mom decided to have her knee partially replaced. The orthopedic surgeon was cocky, and diminished her age. Her second stroke was within four months of the first surgery.

Mom's second knee surgery (yes, she desired another one) was five days old when she flung her legs down over the side of the bed and stood up, but only for a second-- down she went. Her femur broke, and she became confined to her new wheelchair friend in a moment.

Stop the drama, engage in those difficult conversations about advance directives now. There was more peace for me when I was confident I knew what she preferred.

—— Practical Tip ——
Caregiver massage

Equipment:
Massage oil (grapeseed, coconut, or olive)

A bliss-filled hour of deep relaxation, working out areas holding stress. This is good for care recipients and yourself. The massage table may be heated, if you like. There are several different massage styles available from most masseuses.

SHIATSU:
Uses pressure points to work out muscle knots, along with your active breathing as the masseuse directs. This is not a relaxing massage, but it is especially useful for athletes and sport injuries.

SWEDISH:
Highly relaxing massage. Communicate to your masseuse if you want a light, medium, or heavy touch, and if you want them to spend more time in an area. I often ask for more time on my forearms and my feet, as they are often tight, needing release. A scalp massage could be added. It is especially good to relieve stress, headaches, and improve circulation.

THAI:
Uses a round, heated muslin-covered ball filled with about six herbs inside. Extremely deep massage, targeting

inflammation and pain-relief. The masseuse will give you the Thai herbal ball to take home with you.

Hot Stone:

Uses ultra-smooth heated rocks and oil. Euphoria and hydration. A smooth rock will be set on your sacral area, which is the best thing ever. It sounds ridiculous, but when the masseuse removes the rock, you will be sad. This massage is the most relaxing for me.

The gentlest massage oils are grapeseed, coconut, and olive oils. They are also great carrier oils for adding a couple drops of an essential oil. Lavender oil is calming, while grapefruit oil is uplifting. Never allow a masseuse to use almond oil, as it is harsh and may cause allergic reactions.

My personal favorite is grapeseed or coconut oil. I like a heated massage with oils, compared to using lotions, which I find colder on my body. The massage is for caregivers and care recipients, and masseuses are open to making any changes you may need.

— Practical Tip —
Caregiver shopping list

Aquaphor– moisture barrier healing ointment; protectant for dry skin, sweaty areas

Deodorant – if need deodorant, search for a low-aluminum one

Dishwashing soap – any brand you use

Hand soap and Hand Sanitizer – any brand you use

CeraVe/Cetaphil – gentle, hydrating lotion for hands and body

No-Rinse Shampoo Cap - when using water is not possible

Silver Minx – a rinse-out hair treatment, preventing gray hair from yellowing

Medicated Shampoo – for dandruff or flaking scalps

No More Tears Shampoo – keeps eyes free from harsh chemicals

O2 monitor – for index finger; to measure oxygen and pulse rate levels within seconds

Blood pressure machine – Fits on wrist or arm. I found the Omni brand reliable.

Temperature monitor – no-touch forehead or wrist

Glucose monitor – Non-painful finger stick instantly monitors glucose level

Baby Wipes – sensitive skin wipes. For Mom, Huggies wipes didn't dry out easily

Elta Wound Gel – extreme healing for bedsores or red spots on pressure-point areas

Nystatin – for yeast infections. Requires prescription. Powder easier to apply than cream.

Paper Towel – any absorbent brand

Oatmeal – sliced banana, fresh blueberries or peach slices make good additions

Carnation Instant Breakfast/Ensure – for nutrition and increasing weight.

Pudding – individual containers

Thick-It – A stir-in powder, if choking on any liquids. Eases swallowing.

Applesauce – plain, unsweetened individual containers

Check out an app called: Think Dirty Shop Clean.[13] It is an easy way to learn what ingredients are in beauty, personal care, and household products, so you can make the best choices for you and your care recipient.

---

13 www.thinkdirtyapp.com

—— Practical Tip ——
Change bedding

Changing bed linens appears an easy task on the surface. It is--if no one is in the bed. However, it's imperative the person lying in bed, possibly 24/7, is comfortable and clean. Here's the method that works best (meaning I already did it the worst way possible, and over time, found the easiest way).

Lay the care recipient flat on their back in bed.

Remove the top sheet, if they are clothed. If they are not clothed, cover them to extend dignity to them.

Go to the right side of the bed and loosen the fitted bottom sheet at the top and foot of the bed. Push it up the care recipient's body.

Place the new fitted bottom sheet at the top corner and foot of the bed and push it up tightly to your care recipient's body.

Go to the other side of the bed and gently roll your care recipient towards you onto their side.

Push the old fitted bottom sheet and the new sheet completely under their back. Gently roll care recipient back to lay flat.

Go to the opposite side and gently roll your care recipient towards you on their side. Pull the old fitted bottom sheet off the bed, and pull the new fitted bottom sheet through.

Gently roll the care recipient flat again.

Secure the new fitted bottom sheet at the top and foot of the bed corners.

Add their blanket and bedspread, moving the care recipient to a comfy position, raising or lowering their head and feet, either manually or with an electric bed. Place their pillow gently into an easy position, supporting their neck.

— Practical Tip —
Church

Church may be an important spiritual and social part of your care recipient's life. Many churches offer an accessible bus at private residences or facilities. Assisted-living facilities offer Bible studies and church services on-site by local pastors or laypeople.

Call their local church for information. Others from the church may visit during the week, if asked. Communion is provided for anyone who wanted to receive it. Mom's church left portable communion when they visited, and I helped her take it when I came to visit.

The denomination may offer to directly visit your care recipient to receive the Sacrament or other meaningful religious traditions.

Tap into the resources they choose and support them, even if you do not agree with their theology. You are not there to judge, but enable your care recipient to connect with their familiar routines, and deepen their spiritual health.

— Practical Tip —
Delegating

Work smart, not more; delegating is critical as a caregiver. Please don't overuse a person. Be creative and hire someone, if needed. I used a simple notebook in Mom's apartment. When visitors came into the room, they wrote the current date and a recap of what happened while they were there. Place a sign next to the notebook, encouraging visitors to write in it. All of Mom's visitors enjoyed writing a note to her in the book, describing how she was feeling that day, or cool conversations.

If caregivers write in a notebook to keep family and other caregivers up-to-date on their shift, place the book in a place the care recipient cannot access. This gives them dignity and respect to not read detailed information on themselves. It may make them feel like a small child.

When dementia is beginning to be present, it may trigger the care recipient towards angst as they may already have trouble understanding things that were easier a year ago. This challenge isn't brain surgery. All it takes is creativity and decisiveness. Don't make decisions harder by agonizing over them. There will be plenty of other more serious decisions to make. If you have more than one sibling who is willing to help, divide the tasks up and work in each person's strengths.

—— Practical Tip ——
Deodorant

Deodorant may no longer be necessary. It is important to wash and dry thoroughly under the care recipient's arms daily, to prevent any buildup of germs. Choose a gentle, skin-friendly deodorant. Use sparingly or not at all, if odor is no longer a challenge.

— Practical Tip —
Detail organizing

Doctors often know which medications to prescribe. That is the easy part. However, you are the caregiver and you know how the care recipient's health is, day after day. You know when there is a need for medication, less medication, or different medication.

"Kay Nell, your mom is biting at the caregivers."

A caregiver called me one evening.

"What?!"

"She's biting when anyone tries to get close to her."

"That's weird. I'm on my way."

They must be wrong.

When I walked into her apartment, her eyes were wild; as I neared to greet her, she tried to grab my arm and bite me, too. This was new. No attempts soothed her. With a urine stick, I ruled out a UTI (urinary tract infection), which often presented with delusion and hallucination. I called her doctor, and the on-call doctor finally called back about ten in the late evening.

"Well, she does have dementia, and sometimes these things happen."

He rattled on, telling me everything I already knew.

"Please, there has to be some drug that will help her tonight. She wants to bite everyone. No UTI. No TIA. No stroke. Please, isn't there some medication that will help her?"

"Well, there is a drug, but we usually only recommend it for homeless people."

"Well, tonight she is acting homeless!"

He finally agreed to give her a large dose of a new drug to help her sleep, and stop the wild eyes, angry, "I-wanna-bite-you" stage. No pharmacy was open in our area past seven in the early evening. Jordan and I traveled forty-five minutes to an overnight pharmacy for the magic medication. We drove back to administer her medication, traveled fifteen miles home and climbed into bed, exhausted. Within two days Mom's personality was back to herself. She continued on the lowest dose for several years. No delusions ever, or side effects.

I was grateful she was back to kindness and smiles. The principle was to learn the art of negotiating with medical personnel. Do not be intimidated. I knew my care recipient best, and confidence was a necessary trait to exude.

— Practical Tip —
Eyes

Equipment: eye drops, contact lens cleaner, glasses cleaner.

What the care recipient needs will depend on their eye health. If they need cataracts removed, it is quite an easy one-day procedure, with good results for nearly everyone.

Regular assessments of the care recipient's eyes are a must, preferably by an ophthalmologist. Selecting glass frames is the fun part. Lightweight, firm, or soft frames; so many choices. Your care recipient may need your opinion to confirm they are selecting the best glasses.

Contacts come with extra lubrication and could be the best choice for dry eyes. If one brand doesn't work well, try another. Lens cleaners for glasses and contacts are a must. Norwex[14] makes an excellent dry wipe for glasses. It does a perfect job, washable, and lasts well over a year.

---

14 Norwex.com

— Practical Tip —
Finding doctors

Finding the right doctor is an important decision for the health of your care recipient. Does the doctor teleconference? Does the care recipient need to travel to the doctor's office, or will the doctor work with the caregiver or assisted-living facility's RN for basic needs?

At Mom's assisted-living facility, the nurse feared questioning a doctor. She was afraid to be wrong, afraid to advocate for the residents. I considered it ineptness, and called the doctor and his nurse directly. Mom received the care she needed and there was a mutual respect with Mom's medical team.

If you are looking for a new doctor for your care recipient, ask for opinions, and look at Yelp[15] and Healthgrades websites for reviews. Google a potential doctor's name and many resources will come up to help you make the most educated choice.

---

15 Yelp.com, Healthgrades.com, google.com

— Practical Tip —
Games

Equipment:
Deck of playing cards (without the Jokers)

Mom and I were playing Scrabble by the time I was six years old. Sometimes she let me win, but she was competitive, and taught me to increase my vocabulary. As I got older, she taught me to play double solitaire, which was a speedy little game. Did I ever think one day she would not be able to play those games? No. She was losing her ability to plan ahead and her dexterity when I remembered an old card game, War.

Divide a card deck in half. I didn't count the cards out. Give half to the care recipient and half to yourself. Turn over one card each. If the care recipient has the highest card, they win, and take both cards.

Mom could no longer calculate, but she understood high and low cards. I liked the cards messy in front of her because it took the pressure off keeping the cards perfectly in a stack. We played War everywhere: on her wheelchair side table, on a bedside tray, on the dining room table, or anywhere there was a flat surface.

It kept our moments together filled with laughter and activity. The point of playing games was not who won or lost, but it kept her mind (and mine) active. It brought more fun to visits and created a semblance of normality. Okay, I liked to win as much as she did, but I was learning new ways, too.

— Practical Tip —
Hair & Clothing

Equipment:
Dry shampoo cap
Shampoo
Conditioner
Brush or comb

Hair is a frame for the face. Short, medium, or long hair, the process is the same. Short hair is the best possible choice if the care recipient has ambulatory challenges. Short hair is fast to wash and dry. Medium or long hair requires fifteen to thirty minutes more time. Gentle, no-tear shampoo and conditioner work well.

If your care recipient cannot get their hair washed traditionally, the next best thing is the dry shampoo cap. A dry cap has elastic around the edges. Take the cap and place it on the head, like a hair net. Massage their hair through the cap. After a minute or two, remove the cap. The dry shampoo cap is good for one use only. Toss it. The hair will be damp and easy to style with a low setting on a blow dryer. This is a way to clean hair for any other-ability moments.

Even if making choices is limited for the care recipient, they often have a preference. Honor their decision and work with them. Let them choose.

Mom dressed herself. After all, she began dressing herself young, as one of ten siblings. She selected bright colors and patterns. Red in any hue was Mom's favorite. When she married in 1932, she welcomed my dad's clothing styles and color selections, because he had a good eye for design. She, however, was as comfortable in an outfit from a bargain catalog as she was in a Nordstrom best.

Mom was practical. She passed by spa days, and welcomed the chance to help the downhearted. Two years into her health challenges, she wanted me to pick out her clothes. She could still dress herself. I gave her a choice between two outfits so she was in control.

Eventually, she chose not to decide. Every week, I pinned days of the week onto her clothes. I became her hands when she could no longer dress herself. If I wasn't there to dress her, another caregiver knew exactly what she wanted to be dressed in each day.

—— Practical Tip ——
Hoyer[16]

If your care recipient is non-ambulatory, you will be transferring them to chairs, beds, and vehicles. Over time, I found the best way to transfer Mom.

From a chair, I am knee to knee with her. I sometimes use a gait belt around Mom to aid in the lifting and save my back. If without a gait belt, I use the back waist of Mom's pants. I stand knee to her knees to give stability and more control. I bend over, bending my knees, grab the back waist of her pants and lift her up, pivoting her (my feet are in between her feet) and gently seat her on the bed, or chair.

If Mom is in bed, I use the electric bed to raise her head, scooch her feet and buttocks to one side of the bed, place my palm on her back, and lift as I described earlier. Sometimes I place a hoyer net under her, connect the net to the hoyer and lift her by raising the hoyer handle up and down. Be sure the net is under your care recipient's head before raising. Don't ask me how I learned the importance of it.

Hoyers are great for care recipient safety, easy on caregiver backs, and saves time. Power, Manual, Sit-to-Stand and Ceiling hoyers with mesh slings are a few of the options, if it comes time the care recipient needs one. Hoyer netting is available in cotton, polyester, blues, grays, pinks, and in sitting sizes or full-length sizes

---

16 www.rehabmart.com

to lie down. I didn't even know what a hoyer was or how it worked until Mom first needed one.

I chose a Manual hoyer, and pumped a handle to raise Mom with the netting under her body. If your care recipient is non-ambulatory, can stand for limited times, or transferring becomes unsafe for them, the caregiver may need to choose the best hoyer for them to use for years to come. It's a kind, gentle way to move your care recipient from bed to recliner, shower, meals or transporting.

The non-ambulatory care recipient is easy to lift with a hoyer and mesh netting. To wash Mom's hair required two people for safety. One day, we thought outside the box. We placed her head at the foot end of the hoyer netting. It worked well for several years. This made her level with the sink, and we washed her hair with ease. Place a towel under their neck, and they will be at the perfect height by increasing or decreasing the hoyer setting.

A hoyer is easily rolled into a no-lip shower. Turn on the room heat for your care recipient. You may be sweating, but the care recipient's comfort is your first priority, and you can easily cool off later. After the shower, gently dry their body off as much as possible. Drape a large towel over them to offer dignity and respect. Place a couple of towels on the bed to lay the care recipient upon. Remove the netting by rolling gently to each side. It was a workout some days for me, but worth it. Good job!

— Practical Tip —
Incontinence

Equipment:
Adult diapers
Adult pull-ups

There are many degrees of incontinence. If your care recipient is experiencing minor leakage throughout the day, a simple Poise, Always, or similar brand pad will suffice. Incontinence pads are made for males and females. If the leakage is medium or heavy, a better product may be adult pull-ups. They are less bulky and do not show beneath clothes. When Mom was unable to walk to the bathroom in her apartment, a commode by her bed was useful.

If a care recipient is confined to bed most of the day, completely incontinent, an adult diaper with adhesive tabs is a good choice. Pull-ups and adult diapers have a yellow or blue line through the middle of the diaper, changing colors if wet. Wet indicators save skin and time. Most adult diapers are to be changed every two to four hours.

Mom was sent free adult diapers by Medicare. She couldn't maneuver to get one on. She was ambulatory, and the bulky diaper looked hideous on her. I decided to show her how to put one on. I grabbed the diaper through my legs. One adhesive peeled and stuck to my hand, and the other side of the diaper was falling towards the floor. The tabs. The bulk.

Try one on. It changes your perception, coming from the point-of-view of your care recipient, rather than a caregiver view. I gave up and began looking for other options for her. We paid for them, but pull-ups were the ticket; smooth under clothing and easy to use. At this writing, Costco has the best price on all incontinence products.

—— Practical Tip ——
Jewelry & valuables

Eliminate the temptation for others and lock up or take home valuables for safekeeping. When the care recipient no longer appears to care about jewelry, it is a good time to make a safe place for it. If they have piercings, ask if they want to continue wearing the earrings. If they say, "Yes," weekly clean their pierced area with a small cotton swab of rubbing alcohol or hydrogen peroxide (and the backs of the earrings, as well). Infection can occur easily if it's not kept clean.

Mom decided to give me her jewelry for safekeeping when many people came in and out of her room several times a day. Jewelry can be a temptation, and it's respectful to eliminate potential temptation for a person. Hands swell. Rings get tighter. Unplanned hospital admissions happen.

A less expensive jewelry piece can easily be worn and is a more practical choice for some. If it upsets them (and dementia is a piece of the puzzle) leave it on, and let go of the control. Let them make the decision. You will be making much more important decisions than to argue over jewelry they want to wear.

—— Practical Tip ——
Manicures for caregiver

Your hands deserve pampering. Schedule a manicure at a salon. You use your hands daily in a myriad of caregiving tasks. Manicures soften your skin, trim your cuticles, shape your nails, prevent future breakage/splitting, and massage your hands and forearms. If you are okay with the harsher Dremel tool (roughing your nails), you could select gel, solar, or acrylic nails; it takes about one hour. If you want them removed later, a nail technician was best to do it. I've taken them off myself, but it took months for my nails to heal. If the technician removes the special nails, it will take about a month for your nails to return to complete health. A caveat.

— Practical Tip —
Mattress

Your care recipient deserves a great mattress. If they are ambulatory and in bed a few hours overnight, a standard mattress suffices. One-person mattresses are 36" x 80". Non-ambulatory care recipients have several choices to make for a mattress.

The polyurethane mattresses are fluid-proof or resistant, nylon and may contain latex, rubber, or be soy-based. If your care recipient is allergic to latex, secure a hypoallergenic mattress, latex-free. These mattresses are easy to clean and about six inches thick, with one-and-a-half pounds of foam inside.

For pressure-relieving mattresses, they were the same, except the foam was about .3+ denser. There are memory foam mattresses supporting up to a two hundred thirty-pound person, maximum. If the care recipient needs a sturdier mattress, look for a much denser, thicker foam one.

Mattresses are important to the overall health of your care recipient. Assess which mattress is best for your care recipient, and change the mattress type with any health changes.

—— Practical Tip ——
Medications

Perhaps no medications are needed right now. Pick a primary care doctor not requiring excessive office visits especially if they are non-ambulatory. There are some new medications for dementia that may be worth seeking out. Check with the care recipient's doctor for expert opinions and do your own research, as well.

Keep a blood pressure machine, glucose monitor, and an oxygen finger monitor close by, and record the results. This saves time at doctor visits and gives an accurate picture.

When medications are needed, is the care recipient able to take medications on their own? Can they order medication refills? Depending on ability, the caregiver may need to order and administer the medications at the correct time. The caregiver may need to talk with doctors and pharmacists to verify if medications are compatible. Watch for allergies the care recipient may have to medications.

If they are in an assisted-living facility, the nurse handles all medications, refills, and administering them. You can request a record of medications and the time given each day. In the independent apartment side of a facility, the resident is responsible for ordering and administering their own medications.

— Practical Tip —
Mental health evaluation

If a care recipient shows signs of severe depression, hopelessness, or talks about ending their life, it's time to quickly schedule a mental health evaluation. Add in the fact that the care recipient watched many of their friends and family members die.

It would be challenging for most of us, too. If the care recipient's personality changes and becomes uncharacteristically angry, confused, or cannot remember basic things, geriatric evaluations are available at most hospitals, and highly useful.

Since Mom had some dementia, I asked the hospital geriatric evaluators not to tell her where they were from as they evaluated her in her apartment, due to agitation. They said they had to wear their name tags only, and I knew Mom would not notice their name tags--and she didn't.

She answered their questions and enjoyed meeting them. It was best for me not to be present the day of the evaluation. I knew I would want to fill in the blanks in her mind for her, and it would be too emotional for me to watch.

With Mom, I used the information for my own knowledge. I knew where her mind was missing pieces, and I helped her better. The evaluations were done for-your-information only. Depending on the evaluation, you will know what to do or not do and any resources to research. There is also in-hospital evaluations, if needed.

— Practical Tip —
Money

Your care recipient may be overly concerned about money, and if they have enough to pay their way. A family member may be tempted to use the care recipient's money unwisely. I kept a running total of expenditures and income, so if I was ever asked, my conscience was clear.

"Kay Nell, do I have enough money to live here in my apartment, and buy what I need? I don't want you to use your money. Do I have enough?"

"Sure, Mom. You have plenty of money. No worries there."

I could tell she was having an open window from dementia; she always paid her way when managing a business. The truth was, a one-bedroom apartment in her assisted-living facility, nurse availability, bathing, three hot meals, medication disbursement, and housekeeping were at a base of $5,500/month.

Five months prior, Mom's money ran out. We covered the $5,500, plus extras Medicare did not pay. After several months, due to serious caregiver safety issues arising within the facility, she moved about a quarter-mile away into another, safer, assisted-living facility.

Eventually, we implemented Medicaid for Mom. We were still responsible for purchasing many extra supplies, however. If dementia or limited mental capacity is present, please assure them all is well. I knew Mom would worry and possibly give up if she thought she could not pay her way. The dementia had arrived. She would never look at things in the same light again.

— Practical Tip —
Nutrition[17]

Equipment (optional):
Potassium-rich food
Kefir
Vitamin D
Vitamin B12, sublingual
Vitamin C/Zinc
High-protein food

Nutrition is important for a care recipient and caregiver, at any age. Here are some products to think about, which worked well for Mom.

Kefir: A cultured, fermented drink, like thick yogurt. A mega-probiotic for gut health.

Potassium: An essential mineral regulating fluid, muscles, and nerves. Sweet potatoes, beets, Swiss chard, white beans, and bananas are high in potassium.

Vitamin D: Helps the body absorb calcium for muscles and nerves to function well. Fights off bacteria and viruses. Especially useful if living in a less sunny climate.

---

17 Ods.od.nih.gov/factsheets

Vitamin C: Increases collagen and supports wound healing. Kiwi, orange, grapefruit, cantaloupe, and strawberries are the highest in Vitamin C.

Protein: Great for nails and hair; building blocks for bones, muscles, cartilage, skin, and blood. Egg whites, tofu, lean meats, beans, vegetarian meats, Ensure, Carnation Instant Breakfast and Premier Protein drinks are higher in protein.

Please consult your physician before making any changes in nutrition.

—— Practical Tip ——
Oxygen

Please check with the care recipient's doctor if oxygen is needed.

Wheelchair oxygen is an interesting beast. Oxygen tanks are brought in by a company that specializes in oxygen. Find the closest one in your area. Small oxygen tanks are good for traveling outside the home. A round metal oxygen tank holder can be installed on the back of a wheelchair.

There are oxygen tanks with handles and rolling wheels, if your care recipient is steady on their feet. The tanks are not heavy to push. Another option is an even smaller oxygen tank, slung over the shoulder with a soft handle, and carried like a purse or man bag.

Lifting the oxygen tank into the wheelchair holder is no small feat. The tank lasts long enough for an all-day outing. However, if you are pushing the wheelchair with the oxygen tank on the back, it may get in the way of your steps. I bruised my shins when the oxygen tank holder interfered with walking behind the wheelchair. A smaller tank and tank holder is a better solution.

Check the oxygen level on the regulator dial near the tank top to assure a full tank before an outing. The oxygen companies deliver multiple tanks of oxygen. I stored full tanks on the left side of Mom's entry closet, and empty ones on the right with a sign "empty." The company automatically picks up the empty tanks and replaces them with full tanks.

CONCENTRATOR OXYGEN

Although oxygen is something you cannot see, it is a noisy machine. Not intimidating for adults, but children often find it scary. My young Jordan was uncomfortable with the swishing sound, but I was accustomed to it.

There are many increasing levels of caregiving. What is once difficult to accept becomes second nature later. If there are oxygen hoses, one way to contain them is running them under a rubber-backed rug, to prevent people from stepping on or tangling up in them.

Concentrators are about two feet high, and easy to use at home. An oxygen concentrator tank pumps oxygen through the hose, into the cannulas to the care recipient's nose or mouth. If they are a mouth breather, oxygen goes into their mouth. If a nose breather, it goes into their nose.

Always replace the nose cannulas tubing (unscrews from the tube connecting to the concentrator). The nose cannulas tubing can become unsanitary. Wipe the cannulas often with a sanitizing wipe (baby wipes work great). Check the nose cannulas often; though they may be clean, the plastic tubing can harden and hurt the nose, causing skin problems. Ensure the cannulas are soft and pliable.

The goal of the oxygen concentrator is to make life easier. Following simple cleaning assures a higher quality of living. Cleaning concentrators is easy. Remove the square foam piece on the back of the concentrator. Wash by hand with soap and water until the water runs clean through it. Let it dry. Replace it onto the back of the machine. The only thing left to clean is the oxygen tubing. Unscrew the tubing from the machine. Replace the entire tubing if the tubing becomes foggy or hard. Use a portable oxygen tank, if needed, to continue oxygen to the care recipient while cleaning the concentrator.

Directions are usually included when delivered.

— Practical Tip —

Pedicure

Equipment:
Bath towel
Hand towel
Washcloth
Toenail clippers
Gentle manicure file
Plastic orange stick
Nail polish remover
Nail cuticle clipper
Nail filler polish
Nail polish
Quick-dry enamel spray
Foam toe separators
Electric heated foot spa bath or a plastic tub
Latex-free gloves

Pedicure locations: Salon, caregiver at home, Podiatrist, friend, family member

What a wonderful treat for your care recipient and you, their caregiver! Why a pedicure? If a salon visit is the choice, the care recipient is completely in charge of their pedicure. If foot neuropathy is a challenge, the soaking water is easily corrected for temperature.

Look at the salon menu to select one of the pedicure options. The general purpose of a pedicure is removing dead skin (exfoliation), cutting toenails to their healthiest, hydrating skin, and massaging feet and calves. Bring flip-flops or open-toed sandals, if you plan to use nail polish. They will offer you paper-thin flip-flops, but walking in them may be difficult.

The best way I pampered Mom's feet was asking her to sit in her favorite chair: her electric lift chair. She slouched to the side in her chair at times, so I propped up each side of her with pillows and created a stable posture. I placed the electric foot massage tub under her feet. Mom was 5'3", and a stack of books under the massage tub brought her feet and knees up to a comfortable position. Improvise.

Fill the tub with warm water, using a pitcher. If a spa bath massager is used, begin heating the spa and check for a comfortable temperature. The skin of the feet can be tender and sensitive.

Caution: Do not turn on the massage rollers until you try it on your own feet! Some spas have extremely aggressive rollers, and may damage the care recipient's feet (and perhaps your own). Place both feet in the water for five to ten minutes. Mom often went to sleep at this point. When soaking is complete, remove the spa bath and empty in the sink. Clean it after the pedicure is complete.

Put on plastic, latex-free gloves for cleanliness. It helped to remove myself a little from the task, to a more professional level. Place a bath towel over your knee. Lift one foot out of the tub while the other continues soaking, and place on your knee. With the washcloth, begin gently rubbing the bottom of the foot. Dead skin loosens with gentle rubbing. Work between the toes.

Look for infections in between each toe. Epsom salt in a warm water soak is soothing and could draw out infection. If you do find infections or in-grown nails, it's good to see a podiatrist.

After removing the dead skin, pick up the plastic orange stick and gently clean under toenails and push back the cuticles of the nail. Use the cuticle nail clipper to carefully clip any dead skin. If the soak is long enough, you'll see dead skin coming from under the nails. Use the orange stick to gently clean each toe. Wipe off the stick on the bath towel between nails, if needed.

With the nail clippers, clip the toenails, not getting too close to the skin underneath, and not too close in the corners of the nail, as it may irritate the skin. File any roughness on the nail end gently. When done, clean off both feet with a damp washcloth.

Dry thoroughly, including between each toe. Place foam toe separators on both feet, in between toes to keep them from touching. If a toenail has ridges or waves, paint nail filler polish onto the nails. Let it dry. Paint toes the nail color your care recipient likes.

"Whichever one you think is best."

You may not see this as making a choice, but they did choose. They chose to let you decide. Celebrate they made a choice!

After painting the toenails, lightly spray the quick dry enamel, as it decreases the drying time by many minutes. There are shellac and nail polishes that dry instantly. It is harder to remove, but works great when the care recipient has a tough time keeping their hands or feet quiet.

Vary the length and completeness of the pedicure according to their stamina. The real purpose of a pedicure, besides the obvious, is the touch, the care, and the love in action with your care recipient. You are kind, fearless and fun. You took the time. Impressive.

—— Practical Tip ——
Phone

It'd be soothing to hear Mom's cheery voice on the phone again. She used a normal touchtone landline. Small cell phones were still a twinkle in an inventor's eyes. Later, she used a phone with extra-large numbers and speed dial numbers for family. She progressed to needing written, how-to directions for using her phone. She called me every day, asked goofy questions, or yelled at me for not coming to see her. I had just left, and was with her nearly every day.

She instructed me on real estate business deals she did in the past. I stepped into her world often when she was somewhere else in her mind. For a while, I fought it when dementia took her to another time or a make-believe zone. Month by month, it dawned on me to welcome her perceptions, and enjoy full-blown conversations wherever she was in her mind. There was more peace in my heart as I went into her world and connected with her.

There came a time she no longer could hold a phone, dial it, or request paid caregivers to call me, if I wasn't there. It all tapered off gradually, and snuffed out. She was frustrated when she could not remember who she was, whom she loved, her career, and who came to see her in a day. I typed in a large font on paper, laminated and wrote who she was, whom she loved, her career successes, and who came to see her daily. Caregivers and I read it to her when she was confused. We became her memory, and those were priceless moments: to see the sun gradually rise in her eyes as she remembered people and places.

After 9/11 happened, I went to see Mom immediately. She was in bed with a broken femur after knee replacement surgery. I saw that if I told her what was happening in the world, it would make her day too heavy. She cared about things in front of her. Nothing more. Not even the weather.

She became like a young child in her thoughts, completely trusted, depended and relied on me. She was Mom, but the doors were gently closing on vigorous discussions with her. I said goodbye to yet another connection with her.

She was my parent. I helped her through long winter days. Truthfully for me, I felt lonely without the safe ground we once shared. More and more often, sadness seeped in as I drove home, and tears ran free down my face.

Bottomline, enjoy the phone calls now, even if they are multiple, inconvenient times. Savor those conversations.

—— Practical Tip ——
Popcorn balls

Equipment:
1 extra-large bowl
Butter
Plastic wrap
Latex-free gloves
1 large spoon
2-quart kettle

Recipe:
16 cups popped popcorn
1 cup white granulated sugar
2 cups light corn syrup
1 6-ounce box bold-color Jell-O (not sugar free)

Bring sugar and syrup to a strong, rolling boil in a two-quart kettle. Add Jell-O powder and dissolve. Pour slowly over popcorn in a buttered, extra-large bowl. Stir well with a large, buttered spoon to coat the popcorn. Let the popcorn sit for five minutes. Lay out plastic wrap pieces to wrap popcorn balls. Put on latex-free gloves. Butter hands well. Begin pressing popcorn balls together firmly. Tightly wrap in plastic wrap as quickly as possible. Set aside. Makes 18-20 popcorn balls

Mom made hundreds of colorful popcorn balls during the Christmas holidays, delivered to friends and family. When she didn't have the stamina she once did, in her mind she saw herself with stamina. Ask someone how old they feel, and you'll usually hear ten to twenty-five years younger. In her mind, Mom was in her sixth decade, rather than her physical eighth decade.

Close to Christmastime, I helped her into a chair, with her young grandson, Jordan, seated next to her. Pop! Pop! Pop! The aroma wafted through the air. In front of her, I dribbled the syrup across the popcorn and began to stir the syrup into every kernel. I helped Mom butter her hands. Jordan and I followed suit. She started pushing the popcorn together into a ball, as she'd done for nearly fifty years.

Mom thoroughly enjoyed watching Jordan make popcorn balls. She made one popcorn ball the entire day, as she loved watching Jordan make them. She laughed and watched Jordan as if everything was normal, and she was doing the activity herself. Dementia was far from normal. After we were done, I helped her to our reclining leather loveseat, where she fell fast asleep with our brown, short-haired dachshund, Lili, snuggled up beside her. Priceless.

— Practical Tip —
Positioning care recipient

Lower the hospital bed at the head and feet. It was easy with two people, but I will teach you how to do it with one person.

Stand at the head of the bed. Lean over and grab the top of the quilted underpad on each side and gently pull the care recipient towards the head of the bed until within one to two inches near the headboard. You may need to reposition the quilt under the buttocks of the care recipient.

—— Practical Tip ——
Resources

Local Department of Aging offices in most cities have files on all assisted-living facilities, rehab facilities, and nursing home facilities. The files are available to the public. All complaints and results are listed. The files are often mega-enlightening.

No one may want to admit it, but money is a huge factor when exploring resources. The more money, the more options the care recipient may choose. There are other resources if the care recipient is on Medicaid or indigent. As a caregiver, remember there are many different paths to choose, so think outside the box. Brainstorm. Explore logical and creative options. Then choose. You are exercising deep courage and pushing through the tough decisions.

—— Practical Tip ——
Room set-up

This sounds easy, but with the space often allowed, a good room set-up can be challenging. Not only does the room need to work for the person, but for caregivers and family. A local moving company brought my five-foot long upright mahogany piano, the one I was hopping up onto the bench at six-years-old to practice. In her living room was my piano, loveseat, automatic lift chair recliner, and semi-automatic hospital bed, featuring a pressure-relieving mattress. The kitchen counter had the caregiver log-in sheets for the two-hour checks. A notebook for visitors and family to write in after visiting was in the same area.

The best hospital bed is fully automatic. The head and foot raises, and the bed height, as well. Insisting on this type of bed saves your back, as you will be bending over the bed often. If there are diaper changes, catheters, bedsores or quilted underpad changes, you will seriously appreciate the electric height up and down feature. Negotiating with insurance and medical companies for the best bed is worth the time. Please note; talking the language of insurance will be the difference between a manual bed and an electric, fully automatic bed.

— Practical Tip —
Safety

A caregiver keeps their care recipient as safe as possible. If they cannot push a button, use wristbands or neck straps to push for help. If they cannot arise alone from a chair or bed, there are ankle alarms with a high-pitch siren alert. Personally, I found the alarms dehumanizing and disruptive to Mom, with her off-and-on dementia. An assisted-living facility will encourage alarms, as they fear a lawsuit or being written up by the county or state. Another choice was to connect the call string to their shirt. If they moved forward, it automatically, silently called for a caregiver to assist. A new technology arrived; GPS socks for tracking locations.

There is a huge push in the industry to not allow the use of bedrails. Oregon believes a person's head or body may get stuck between the bedrail and mattress and cause death.[18] My view is it is pretty much about lawsuits. Mom was a fall risk, and several years into my caregiving, the assisted-living facility--instructed by the state--removed all bedrails (although they were okay in nursing homes and hospitals). Mom was more likely to fall out of bed without a rail. I found a good solution for her. Mom was in a bed often; Medicare paid for a deep (5"-8") pressure-relieving mattress. I tied solid foam wedges onto the springs, under the mattress, on each

---

18 https://www.fda.gov/medical-devices/bed-rail-safety/safety-concerns-about-bed-rails

side of the bed. Elevating the mattress on each side, I created a little cocoon to cradle her and keep her from easily falling out of bed.

My elderly father-in-law became a fall risk in an assisted-living facility. Their solution was to put a double mattress down on the floor beside his bed. Although they solved the fall risk, it greatly limited all his walking, and what dignity he had left.

— Practical Tip —
Skin care

Skin care is basic health. Skin often becomes dryer with age, so a good moisturizer is excellent to use daily on face, hands, arms, and legs. Grapeseed or coconut oil with a drop of lavender makes an excellent body lotion. Hydrating CeraVe or other dermatologically-tested lotions work well, too. One item definitely required is Aquaphor.

Aquaphor has a high healing level, in my experience. Aquaphor is the new "Greek window cleaner" (from My Big Fat Greek Wedding movie[19]). It has minerals added in and heals many simple exterior skin issues. It's great to use in skin creases and for diaper rash areas. The contents are petroleum, mineral oil, ceresin, lanolin alcohol, panthenol, glycerin, bisabolol.[20]

Care recipients may tell you the skin lotions they desire. If not, you will need to decide what tender-loving care you are willing to seek out to encourage hydrating their skin.

SUPPLY LIST
Aquaphor
Deodorant
Dish soap
Hand soap
Antibacterial sanitizer

---

19 https://www.youtube.com/watch?v=A0RVkqXuSCM
20 www.AquaphorUS.com

No-rinse shampoo
Oatmeal packets
Pudding
Thick It
Applesauce
Baby wipes
Cetaphil lotion
CeraVe lotion
Medicated shampoo
Elta wound gel
Nystatin powder
Paper towels
Silver Minx (prevents white hair from yellowing)

--- Practical Tip ---
Video cameras

The latest and greatest camera for the early 2000s I took home, viewed it on my computer, returned it to Mom's room, and reset it for recording. It had night vision, but no sound.

I highly recommend installing a hidden camera, as there are many levels of caregiving, and part of your caregiving role is to protect and advocate for your care recipient, especially when they cannot communicate well.

If in a facility or in a home, set up a video camera with night vision and voice 24/7. It can connect to your phone. A camera saves you many hours of uncertainty, alleviates stress, and increases safety for your care recipient. Enjoy selecting the best one for your situation. It's one simple way you care-give for your care recipient, especially if they do not have a voice any longer or become easily confused. You need to be their voice.

You are spending so much time getting to know details about your care recipient, you know exactly what they would say or do. You are their voice, their advocate, and it is a high responsibility. Do it with integrity and clarity. Protect them.

ACKNOWLEDGEMENTS

Phil, the love of my life. You consistently offer me grace, mercy, deep love, and laughter for nearly fifty years. You are my steady rock.

Jordan and Nicole—son and daughter-in-love—you listen to me, you believe in me, you trust me, and you always have my back. You love me excellently. You see me and know me.

Jim and Cheryl Boyd—my brother and sister-in-love— for your optimistic spirits, openness, and encouraging words.

My new writing friends around the world made the last few years the best time ever.
Lyla Peterson and Lynn Saint, USA
Isabel Baker and Mish Graham, Australia
Linda Powell, New Zealand

Nika Maples, my mentor and teacher; you are a hope giver.

CPSIA information can be obtained
at www.ICGtesting.com
Printed in the USA
BVHW081058100222
628583BV00007B/181